Leading With Heart

OrangeBooks Publication

1st Floor, Rajhans Arcade, Mall Road, Kohka, Bhilai, Chhattisgarh 490020

Website: **www.orangebooks.in**

© Copyright, 2024, Author

All rights reserved. No part of this book may be reproduced, stored in a retrieval system, or transmitted, in any form by any means, electronic, mechanical, magnetic, optical, chemical, manual, photocopying, recording or otherwise, without the prior written consent of its writer.

First Edition, 2024

ISBN: 978-93-6554-766-5

LEADING WITH HEART

The Transformative Power Of Servant Leadership

PARTHIBAN RAMASAMY

OrangeBooks Publication
www.orangebooks.in

This book is dedicated to my parents, Ramasamy Chettiar and Thangammal (Lakshmi), as well as my grandmother, Chinnammal.

Introduction

The world is changing fast, and leadership is changing right along with it. People are starting to question traditional leadership styles that focus on power, control, and strict hierarchies. Instead, a new way of leading is taking over - one that puts people first and values empathy, teamwork, and support. This new way of thinking about leadership is all about servant leadership. It flips the script on traditional norms by putting the needs of others first.

"Leading with Heart: The Transformative Power of Servant Leadership" explores how this approach can truly make a difference in people's lives. This book doesn't just offer guidance; it challenges leaders at all levels to embrace a mindset that prioritizes their teams. By creating an environment where individuals feel valued and empowered, leaders can inspire their teams to excel, think creatively, and perform at their best. Through case studies, research, and personal narratives, this book delves into the core principles and practices of servant leadership. It shows how qualities like empathy, humility, and honesty can positively impact organizational culture and lead to long-term success.

Readers will discover the benefits of embracing a servant leadership approach, which can assist in reaching goals, increasing productivity, and improving employee morale. Let's delve further into what servant leadership means.

Contents

Introduction v

Chapter - 1
Introduction to Servant **Leadership** 1

Chapter - 2
The Servant Leader Mindset 14

Chapter - 3
Practical Strategies for Servant Leadership 25

Chapter - 4
Cultivating a Positive Work Culture 38

Chapter - 5
Emotional Intelligence in Leadership..........................50

Chapter - 6
Building Trust with Your Team 61

Chapter - 7
Case Studies of Successful Servant Leaders..............71

Chapter - 8
Servant Leadership in Personal Life 82

Chapter - 9
Ethical Implications of Servant Leadership 92

Chapter - 10
Promoting Collaboration and Teamwork 103

Chapter - 11
Developing Effective Communication Skills......... 113

Chapter - 12
　Fostering Innovation and Creativity 125

Chapter - 13
　The Future of Servant Leadership 136

Chapter - 14
　Measuring the Impact of Servant Leadership 148

Chapter - 15
　Conclusion and Next Steps 159

Chapter - 1
Introduction to Servant Leadership

Defining Servant Leadership

Servant leadership is a standout concept in the world of leadership because it prioritizes the needs of others. This approach challenges the typical power dynamics by focusing on the growth and well-being of team members. It goes beyond just managing tasks and highlights the importance of trust, empathy, and genuine care.

Servant leadership revolutionizes the traditional top-down leadership model by distributing power throughout the entire organization, rather than concentrating it at the top. A servant leader's primary responsibility is to support their team by providing the necessary resources, guidance, and encouragement for success. This style of leadership fosters a team-oriented atmosphere, encourages innovation, and ensures that everyone feels valued and appreciated.

The idea of servant leadership has old roots going back to ancient writings and beliefs. But Kumar K. Greenleaf brought this idea to today's world. In his influential article, "The Servant as Leader," Greenleaf emphasized that a true leader must prioritize serving others. This concept challenges the traditional notion of leadership as merely a position of authority and dominance. Instead, it highlights leadership as a means of caring for others, with the leader nurturing the team's well-being and development.

A servant leader has a bunch of important traits, but empathy is the most crucial. Empathy means you can understand and share how others feel. When leaders empathize with their team, they can handle issues and problems with care and intelligence. This caring approach helps build strong trusting bonds, which are essential for any team's success.

Another important aspect of servant leadership is being humble. Servant leaders don't seek attention for themselves. Instead, they take pride in their team's accomplishments. They're willing to admit when they're wrong and are open to learning from others, no matter their position in the organisation. This down-to-earth approach creates an environment where everyone respects each other and continues to grow.

Listening is also a key component of servant leadership. Good leaders pay close attention to their team and value their input. This not only makes people feel included but also leads to better decisions. When team members know they're being heard, they tend to be more devoted to achieving shared goals.

Servant leaders also focus on helping their team member's growth and improvement. They invest time and resources in mentoring, coaching, and providing opportunities for advancement in both work and personal life. This commitment to developing people goes beyond just building skills; it involves supporting the whole person. These leaders understand that overall well-being is connected to success at work.

Servant leadership can be seen in leaders who prioritize clear communication, accessibility, and approachability. They create a safe space for trying new things and learning from mistakes. Companies that embrace servant leadership value collaboration over competition and prioritize team success over personal recognition.

Servant leadership is a demanding yet invaluable approach to leadership. It necessitates a deep commitment to others, a readiness to prioritize their needs above your own, and the courage to be vulnerable while still guiding. However, the rewards for both the leader and their team are significant. By leading with empathy, servant leaders create environments where people feel supported, valued, and motivated to excel in their work.

Historical Context and Evolution

The concept of compassionate leadership goes way back to old societies. Back then, people looked up to their leaders as guides for how to behave and treat others. Take ancient Egypt, for example. Pharaohs weren't just rulers - they were also seen as holy shepherds. Their job was to look after their people's well-being. This way of leading was tied to what they believed in religion and culture. These beliefs put a lot of weight on being caring, fair, and doing the right thing.

When Ashoka the Great ruled ancient India, leadership changed a lot. After a time of harsh conquests, Ashoka became a Buddhist and started to lead in a new way. He focused on peace, kindness, and taking care of his people. He had his ideas carved on pillars and rocks. These writings pushed for fair rule, stood up for animal rights, and backed programs to help society. This set an example for future rulers who wanted to lead with understanding and do what's right. Today, Ashoka's story still pushes leaders to put their people first and rule with heart.

In ancient Greece, famous thinkers like Plato and Aristotle looked at what makes a good leader. Plato's idea of the philosopher-king in The Republic stressed how important wisdom, justice, and working for everyone's benefit are for a leader. On the other hand, Aristotle, in his Nicomachean Ethics, highlighted that being good and acting is key in leadership. He believed leaders should set a moral example to inspire and uplift their followers.

The Mahabharata shows servant leadership through characters like Lord Krishna and Yudhishthira. This leadership style prioritizes the well-being of others and follows moral principles rather than focusing on personal benefits. Krishna takes on the role of Arjuna's charioteer and offers guidance in the Bhagavad Gita showing selfless leadership. In the same way, Yudhishthira shows kindness and feels responsible for his people. The epic teaches us that real leaders give power to others, set good examples, and serve with humility and honesty.

In the Bible, Jesus shows what servant leadership looks like. He teaches and practices being humble and serving others. He stresses that true greatness comes from helping other people. The Apostle Paul also lives out this idea. He calls himself a servant of Christ Jesus. This points out how important it is to be selfless and committed to God and others. These lessons highlight that serving is more important than being served. This approach helps create teamwork and success in different settings.

The Industrial Revolution and the rise of corporate leadership that followed brought new tests and chances for leaders to show compassion. Indra Nooyi, who used to run PepsiCo, showed how to mix servant leadership with being assertive. She made major choices like buying Tropicana and joining Quaker Oats. Though she was assertive, she stayed true to herself, and people saw her as a leader who changed things. Similarly, Satya Nadella, the CEO of Microsoft, also leads in this manner. He gets people to work together through "One Microsoft" and lets workers come up with new ideas and include everyone. This has helped make the organisation do well.

In today's world civil rights movements and the fight for social justice have had a large impact on how we see caring leaders. People like Mahatma Gandhi, Martin Luther King Jr., and Nelson Mandela showed us what it means to lead with understanding, strength, and a strong belief in fairness and justice for all. Their examples continue to inspire today's leaders to prioritize human dignity and social responsibility above all else.

Leadership has evolved significantly in today's interconnected world, where we are confronted with major problems such as climate change, income inequality, and social justice. Leaders across various fields must now prioritize empathy, ethical decision-making, and accountability towards both individuals and the environment. This highlights the crucial role of compassion and adaptability in navigating the challenges of a constantly changing world.

Core Principles

Good leadership is built on key principles that influence actions, decisions, and relationships. These principles aren't just abstract theories; they are practical guidelines that drive leadership daily. They are the foundation of a leader's character, affecting how they inspire, guide, and connect with their teams.

One of the most important things about being a good leader is being authentic. When leaders are true to themselves, they can gain the trust and respect of their team. They don't try to be someone they're not; instead, they show their right personalities. This honesty helps create an environment where team members feel safe sharing their thoughts, concerns, and goals. It also promotes open communication and helps build a culture of honesty and integrity.

Empathy plays a key role in ethical leadership. Leaders who show empathy take the time to grasp their team's feelings and views. They pay close attention and react with kindness. This deep insight helps to build strong bonds within the group. It makes sure choices are made while thinking about how they'll affect each person creating a helpful and caring workplace.

Having a strong vision is crucial for effective leadership. A clear and compelling vision provides guidance and purpose, motivating the team to strive towards shared objectives. Leaders who can articulate their vision in a way that resonates with their team can gather together to achieve their goals. By looking beyond immediate challenges and focusing on long-term objectives, visionary leaders keep their teams motivated and aligned.

In today's ever-changing world of leadership, being able to adapt is essential. Leaders must be flexible and open to change, ready to adjust their plans and methods when new information arises or circumstances shift. This flexibility not only helps navigate uncertainties but also demonstrates to the team that change is a natural part of growth and can be managed effectively. It fosters an environment where fresh ideas and continuous improvement can flourish.

Taking responsibility is a key principle that emphasizes the importance of owning up to our actions and results. Great leaders make sure to hold themselves and their team accountable for what they do and achieve. This principle helps create a culture of trust and reliability within the team. When leaders show accountability, they set a high standard for everyone else, encouraging a sense of responsibility and motivation to aim for excellence.

Inclusivity plays a key role in building a unified and energetic team. Leaders who embrace inclusion appreciate diversity and make sure everyone's ideas get attention and respect. They go out of their way to find different viewpoints and give everyone a chance to pitch in. This approach not only makes decision-making better but also helps team members feel like they belong and are treated.

Resilience stands out as a vital feature of good leadership. Leaders with resilience stay committed and calm when things get tough. They bounce back from problems while keeping a positive attitude. This toughness builds confidence and determination in the team pushing them to tackle obstacles and keep their eyes on the result.

By implementing these significant ideas, leaders can establish a positive and motivating work environment where employees feel valued, motivated, and engaged. These ideas are not rigid; they evolve as you gain experience and dedicate time to reflection, influencing a leader's growth and the team's overall success. Effective leadership involves a continuous exchange of these guiding principles, with each one reinforcing the others to foster a cohesive team that collaborates effectively and achieves goals together.

Benefits of Servant Leadership

Servant leadership has a transformative impact on people's lives and contributes to creating a more just and compassionate world. This leadership style offers numerous benefits to both leaders and their organizations. At its core, servant leadership prioritizes the needs of team members, fostering a culture of mutual respect and collaboration.

One great thing about being a servant leader is that it boosts employee engagement and happiness at work. When leaders genuinely care about their team's well-being and development, it fosters loyalty and commitment. This results in employees feeling valued and respected, leading to lower attrition rates and a more stable organization.

Servant leadership is the secret ingredient that takes work to the next level. When leaders prioritize their team and foster a culture of respect and collaboration, amazing things happen. It not only improves efficiency and boosts productivity, but also enhances the overall work environment.

One of the coolest things about servant leadership is how it empowers team members. By giving them more control and encouraging self-reliance, leaders help their teams unleash their creativity and come up with awesome new ideas. This creates a setting where everyone feels comfortable sharing their thoughts and taking charge of their work.

And let's not forget about problem-solving. Servant leadership values different viewpoints and encourages teamwork, which leads to more effective solutions. Teams become like a tight-knit family, working together towards a common goal with a shared vision.

So, if you want to make a tangible difference in your organization and beyond, embrace servant leadership. It's like the superhero cape your team never knew they needed.

Servant leadership plays a significant role in the personal development of team members. Leaders who use this style focus on being mentors and coaches. They assist their employees in advancing their careers and acquiring new skills. Investing time and effort into fostering the team's growth not only benefits the employees but also enhances the overall strength of the organization. When employees continue to learn and adapt, they become more adept at handling challenges and new issues that arise.

The ethical side of servant leadership plays a key role and we shouldn't take it. When leaders put others' needs first, they show integrity and ethical behaviour setting an example for everyone in the organisation and creating an atmosphere of trust and openness. If workers see their bosses being honest and fair, they're more likely to follow these traits in their jobs. This ethical approach can boost the organisation's image building trust with customers, partners, and the community at large.

Servant leadership has a significant impact on shaping organizational culture. It fosters an environment where people collaborate and support each other. This approach inspires employees to offer a helping hand and work together towards common goals, strengthening the sense of community within the organization. When employees feel supported in this way, they tend to be happier in their roles and have an overall better experience. They feel valued and part of a strong team.

The influence of servant leadership extends beyond the organization's boundaries. By promoting a culture of care and respect, these leaders contribute to creating a caring and more unbiased society. Companies that embrace servant leadership are more likely to engage in social responsibility initiatives and make a positive impact in their communities. This focus on helping others not only enhances the organization's reputation but also instils a sense of pride and purpose in employees.

At its essence, servant leadership affects various aspects that are not immediately visible. When leaders prioritize their team's needs and development, they cultivate a dynamic, ethical, and innovative workplace culture. This leadership style not only enhances individual and team performance but also fosters trust and transparency within the organization. The effects of servant leadership permeate throughout the organization and beyond, establishing a profound and impactful way of leading.

Common Misconceptions

Many people mistakenly believe that leading with heart means being overly emotional or weak. This misconception comes from the idea that being emotionally intelligent and empathetic is a sign of weakness. However, leading with heart doesn't mean letting your emotions get in the way or being a pushover. It's about striking a balance between compassion and assertiveness. It involves understanding others while also making firm decisions and setting boundaries.

Another misconception is that leaders who show compassion care less about achieving results than those who use traditional methods. This belief implies that a kind approach to leadership prioritizes team member's well-being over meeting organizational goals. However, in reality, leaders who demonstrate empathy and compassion often cultivate more loyalty, inspire greater creativity, and enhance productivity within their teams. When individuals feel valued and heard, they are more likely to become actively engaged and dedicated to their work, resulting in improved outcomes.

Some individuals believe that leading with heart is an innate quality that one either possesses or lacks. This notion fails to recognize that emotional intelligence can be developed. Just as one can enhance technical skills through learning and practice, the ability to lead with heart can also be improved. Leadership characteristics are not fixed - they can be improved and refined over time with dedication. By engaging in self-reflection, seeking feedback, and remaining open to learning, leaders can enhance their ability to connect with others on a deeper level.

Many people assume that heart-centred leadership is only suitable for certain professions or industries, such as non-profits or social work. This limited perspective overlooks the potential for leading with a heart to be beneficial in any sector. Whether in large corporations, new tech startups, or government agencies, demonstrating empathy, active listening, and genuine care for your team can transform workplace culture and contribute to success. Heart-centred leadership is applicable across all fields and can be adapted to various challenges and circumstances.

One common misconception is that leading with heart means avoiding difficult conversations or running away from disagreements. However, leaders who lead with heart understand the importance of addressing issues directly, but they do so with compassion and respect. They recognize that challenging conversations provide opportunities for growth and improvement for individuals and teams. By approaching conflicts with care, they can navigate these situations in a way that strengthens relationships rather than damaging them.

Some people believe that leading with heart is a solo endeavour, but this overlooks the collaborative nature of heart-centred leadership. It's about creating a work environment where everyone is encouraged to lead with kindness. This fosters a culture where empathy and understanding are not just imposed from above, but are built into the organization's operations. When everyone participates, the principles of heart-centred leadership not only endure but succeed throughout the entire team.

By dispelling these misunderstandings, we can see that leading with heart does not mean sacrificing results or avoiding tough decisions. Instead, it involves incorporating empathy into your leadership style, fostering an environment where mutual respect and understanding are valued. It's about recognizing that taking care of your team and achieving your organization's goals can go hand in hand.

Chapter - 2

The Servant Leader Mindset

Self-Awareness and Reflection

As the soft light of dawn filters through the window, it bathes the room in a warm glow. The leader sits with eyes closed, taking deep breaths. In this peaceful moment, an inner conversation begins to unfold. Ideas, feelings, and thoughts drift through the mind, unveiling self-insights that are often overlooked in the chaos of everyday life. This simple act of introspection lays the foundation for leadership that truly makes an impact.

At the core of good leadership is knowing yourself. Self-awareness isn't just a quality you have - it's something you practice all the time. It means taking a hard honest look at what you're good at where you struggle, what drives you, and what you believe in. It's like peeling an onion removing layers of pretending and ego to find the original of yourself underneath. When leaders are authentic, it allows them to connect with their team on a deeper level, fostering trust and respect.

When things get quiet and you have time to think, you start to see patterns. You look back at the choices you've made and what happened because of them. You figure out what went well and what didn't. You notice what sets you off emotionally and how you react. This isn't about beating yourself up, it's about learning and getting better. You realize that everything that happens good or bad teaches you something important. It helps you to grow as a person and in your job.

As the room fills with the soft hum of morning activity, the leader wakes up feeling a new sense of clarity. This clarity comes from purposeful and thoughtful reflection showing them that real leadership isn't about having all the answers but asking the right questions. What drives me? What do I value most? Do my actions match these values? These questions guide the leader helping them make choices that not only have an impact on others but are also ethical and caring.

The leader is ready to tackle the day with renewed energy. Self-confidence is key in navigating the challenges of leadership with grace and integrity. Knowing oneself lights the path forward and provides stability during difficult times.

The entire day the leader stays in tune with their inner world. They spot when stress starts to sneak in and pause to breathe and reset. They know how their mood and actions affect their team. This focus lets them choose how to act, not just react creating a good and busy place to work.

As the day comes to a close, the leader takes a moment to reflect. They think about the conversations and decisions made throughout the day, identifying successes and areas for improvement. This practice of self-reflection is not just an extravagance - it is essential. It enables the leader to grow and evolve, leading with authenticity and compassion.

Knowing oneself and looking inward form the base of kind and strong leadership. These skills help leaders grasp their minds and, in turn, get and bond with others. By doing this inner work, leaders can inspire, guide, and elevate those around them. This leaves a lasting positive impact and brings about meaningful change.

Empathy and Active Listening

Understanding and appreciating others' perspectives is essential for effective leadership. When a leader takes the time to listen, trust and connection are established. Empathetic leaders go beyond their viewpoint, delving into the emotions and experiences of their team members. This emotional bond fosters an environment where people feel valued and understood.

Imagine a bustling office filled with the sound of keyboards clicking and people chatting, creating an energetic atmosphere of productivity. During all the activity, a boss is engaged in a one-on-one conversation with a team member who appears to be feeling anxious. Instead of immediately jumping in to solve the problem or offering quick reassurances, the boss provides support, makes eye contact, and truly listens. This simple yet significant gesture has the power to completely shift the dynamic of the conversation. The team member feels a sense of relief knowing that their worries have been acknowledged and understood.

Active listening goes beyond just hearing words; it means tuning into the emotions and intentions behind what's being said. A leader's body language, facial expressions, and verbal cues all play a role in showing empathy. Thoughtful gestures, an open attitude, and repeating back what you've heard can help strengthen the bond between you and your team. When a leader echoes team member's feelings without judgment or interruption, it creates a safe space for honest conversations to take place.

Empathy in leadership is more than just having one-on-one conversations. It means being able to understand the emotions of the entire team. A great leader can sense when there is hidden stress, quiet victories, and the overall mood of the group. They recognize that each person's experiences contribute to the team's atmosphere. By addressing these subtle issues, they foster an environment where teamwork and respect can thrive.

Imagine a scenario where a group tackles a complicated project. As due dates get closer, tension starts to build. A boss who shows empathy doesn't just ask for results. They see the tension, get where people are coming from, and offer a hand. They might say, "I get that this is a tough time for everyone. Let's put our heads together to figure out how to handle this workload." When you combine these words with genuine empathy, it can ignite the team and transform a daunting job into a shared goal.

Empathy has a major impact on solving conflicts. When people disagree, a leader who cares tries to see all sides before fixing things. They pay attention to what each person worries about, show they understand how they feel, and try to find an answer that respects what everyone thinks. This way of doing things doesn't just solve the problem right now. It also makes the team closer and trust each other more.

In the realm of leadership, empathy and active listening are key players in bringing everything together. They are essential in establishing trust and respect with your team. When you demonstrate empathy and truly listen to your team members, you transform from just a boss to a mentor and a friend. You understand their perspective and support them in reaching their full potential. By being empathetic and a good listener, you not only accomplish your leadership goals, but you also cultivate a motivated team that is capable of overcoming any challenge that comes their way.

Humility and Authenticity

As the gentle morning light filters in, you begin to understand the essence of a real leader. It's not about flashy displays or great talk, but a consistent serving of humility. This trait, often underestimated in today's leadership guide, forms the foundation for establishing trust and gaining respect. Leaders who remain humble recognize their boundaries and appreciate the contributions of others. Instead of trying to outshine their team with their intelligence, they choose to guide everyone towards success.

In leadership, humility shows up when you listen more than you talk and learn more than you teach. Being a humble leader means acknowledging your weaknesses and having the courage to admit when you make a mistake. A humble leader doesn't avoid vulnerability; they embrace it as a strength. This fosters an environment where team members can freely share their ideas and concerns without worrying about retaliation. Being open like this helps cultivate a culture that is constantly improving and generating fresh ideas. It allows the best ideas to shine through, regardless of where they originate from.

Authenticity goes hand in hand with humility showing leaders the way to stick to their values and principles. True leaders don't put on masks or act to fit what people think a leader should be. They're honest, open, and steady in what they do and decide. This reality clicks with their teams building the trust that's key for good leadership.

A true leader's actions align with their words, reflecting their core values. This consistency between beliefs and behaviour builds trust among team members, as they can predict their leader's honesty. Being genuine doesn't mean being flawless; it means being authentic and approachable. This quality helps leaders form genuine connections with their teams, fostering a sense of belonging and mutual respect.

In real life, you can't just turn humility and authenticity on and off whenever you feel like it. These qualities are essential parts of a leader's personality, developed through self-reflection and personal growth. Leaders who focus on cultivating these traits often find that their teams are more loyal and committed. They understand that leadership isn't about giving orders, but about supporting others in reaching their full potential.

When humility and authenticity work together, they create a strong team dynamic. Humble leaders give credit where it's due and recognize what their team members bring to the table. At the same time, authentic leaders make sure their praise is real and from the heart. This mix gives team members a sense of purpose and belonging pushing them to do their best work and team up.

As the day goes on and problems come up, the modest and true leader stays strong. They handle obstacles and always consider how their actions impact the team. They enjoy wins together and see failures as chances to learn. By setting an example, they create a culture of modesty and honesty in their organisation making sure these values are real every day, not just something to aim for.

Ultimately, effective leadership is characterized by the humble strength of modesty and the consistent power of authenticity. These traits, while not impressive, make a lasting impact on those who have the privilege of witnessing them in action.

Commitment to the Growth of Others

Leading with Heart is a book that delves into the essence of leadership. It emphasizes the significance of leaders displaying kindness, empathy, and emotional intelligence. The book explores how leaders can inspire their teams, foster growth, and empower them to achieve greatness. This fosters an environment where everyone can thrive and excel. It serves as a guide for individuals who aspire to lead with both their intellect and their emotions. The ultimate objective? To cultivate workplaces where individuals feel valued and motivated to give their best effort.

In servant leadership, the commitment to the growth of others is at the core of the leader's philosophy. Instead of focusing solely on their success and advancement, servant leaders prioritize the development and well-being of their team members. This means providing mentorship, guidance, and support to help them reach their full potential. By investing in the growth of others, servant leaders create a positive work environment where employees feel valued and empowered. This ultimately leads to higher levels of employee satisfaction, engagement, and productivity. In essence, servant leadership is all about lifting others and helping them succeed – because when your team thrives, so does the organization as a whole.

Leaders should lead by example by practicing what they preach. Demonstrating a commitment to self-improvement inspires team members to do the same. This includes being receptive to feedback, continuously learning, and remaining resilient in challenging situations. A leader who exhibits these qualities motivates their team to embrace a similar attitude towards personal growth.

Building Community
The heart of good leadership isn't just about getting results. It's also about creating a feeling of togetherness and belonging in a team. Leaders who care understand that building a workplace community is key to success, both for individuals and the group. This way of leading does more than just manage people. It connects with how people feel and interact making a workplace where everyone supports and works together.

Imagine walking into an office filled with positive energy and good vibes. The coworkers meet each other with genuine smiles, and conversations are filled with respect and support. This kind of atmosphere doesn't just happen by accident - it's the result of hard work to foster a sense of community. A boss who prioritizes this knows the importance of creating an environment where team members feel valued and heard.

A crucial aspect of creating such an environment is open communication. When team members can freely express their thoughts, concerns, and aspirations without fear of judgment, it builds trust. Team meetings, one-on-one discussions, and anonymous feedback channels all contribute to keeping the lines of communication open. People who feel their opinions are valued are more likely to actively participate and take ownership of their work.

Another important element is recognizing and celebrating individual and group achievements. Whether it's a small milestone or a major success, acknowledging these moments fosters a sense of pride and belonging. Simple gestures like sending a congratulatory email, giving public recognition in a meeting, or organizing a small office celebration can boost morale and strengthen the sense of community.

Building a community also involves promoting inclusivity and diversity. A leader who values different perspectives and backgrounds helps create a more innovative and dynamic environment. This means actively seeking out diverse voices and ensuring that everyone has the opportunity to contribute. Inclusivity goes beyond just having a diverse group of people present; it's about creating a space where everyone feels comfortable and empowered to share their unique insights.

Furthermore, empathy plays a crucial role in fostering a sense of community. When you acknowledge and address the emotions of your team members, it strengthens the bonds between them and creates a more cohesive group. This could involve offering support during difficult times, providing opportunities for personal growth, or simply taking the time to listen to individual concerns. Demonstrating empathy shows that the leader values each team member as a whole person, not just as an employee.

To enhance the community spirit, you can also organize team bonding activities outside of regular work duties. Team-building exercises, social gatherings, or casual get-togethers can help team members connect on a personal level. These interactions help to build trust and friendships, making it easier and more effective to collaborate.

The physical office environment also plays a role in fostering team spirit. A welcoming space that encourages interaction can make a significant difference. Well-designed communal areas, team workspaces, and small touches like comfortable seating or shared coffee stations can encourage informal conversations and strengthen relationships.

Leading with compassion means recognizing that a team's strength lies in its unity. By promoting open communication, celebrating achievements, fostering inclusivity, showing empathy, and supporting personal connections, a leader can cultivate a vibrant community. This not only boosts individual morale but also drives collective success, creating a workplace where everyone feels valued and motivated to give their best effort.

Chapter - 3

Practical Strategies for Servant Leadership

Encouraging Collaboration

As you walk through the halls of a successful organization, you can see how collaboration makes a difference. It's the excitement of brainstorming ideas with your colleagues, the satisfaction of working together on a project, and the support you get from your team when you need it. It's all about creating an environment where everyone's voice is heard and everyone's hard work is recognized.

When people come together and combine their efforts, they can achieve more than any one person could on their own. This is something that can't be taught in a class - it's something you see in action every day. A good leader understands the power of collaboration and seeks out partnerships to make it happen.

Building a culture of positive leadership is key to fostering collaboration from the bottom up. Managers need to be humble and open to feedback, creating an atmosphere of openness and tolerance within the organization. When leaders listen to their team and show that they value their input, it creates a sense of inclusion and appreciation that motivates everyone to do their best work.

In the end, a healthy working culture is built on collaboration and recognition. When employees know that their efforts are valued, they are more likely to go above and beyond in their work. So, next time you're working on a project, remember the power of collaboration and how it can make a real difference in the success of your organization.

Leaders need to lead by example and create a work environment that promotes cooperation and collaboration. This can mean having open office spaces without physical barriers, holding more group meetings, and using tools that make it easy for team members to work together. The physical and electronic environment in which teams operate can greatly affect how effective they are.

But it's not just about the environment - recognizing and celebrating team achievements is also key to fostering collaboration. When a project is completed as a team, it's important to acknowledge everyone's contributions. This can be done through rewards, verbal praise in meetings, or written thank-you notes. These gestures show the value of teamwork and encourage further cooperation.

Trust is another crucial aspect of a collaborative culture. Building trust involves open and honest communication, creating a space where team members feel comfortable sharing their thoughts and opinions. Managers can also build trust by being transparent about their challenges and experiences. When team members feel trusted, they are more likely to contribute their best efforts towards achieving common goals. Working together with a team involves more than just getting along - it's about embracing different perspectives and leadership styles. You have to be able to lead group discussions, encourage input from everyone, and guide the team towards reaching a consensus and putting plans into action. It's like being a facilitator, a teacher, and a referee all at once, to keep things on track and everyone on the same page.

When building a team that values collaboration, it's important to recognize that each person brings their strengths and weaknesses to the table. By understanding that everyone has unique talents, leaders can assign tasks that play to each team member's strengths. This not only boosts productivity but also keeps team members satisfied with their work.

Ultimately, teamwork is about creating a sense of unity and shared success. It's about recognizing the value of each team member and their contributions towards a common goal. When everyone feels like they're part of something bigger, that's when the magic happens.

Effective Communication Techniques

Effective communication is essential for successful management and reaching organizational goals. It's not just about sending a message; it's about connecting with and inspiring others. Leaders need to communicate clearly and compassionately to influence and guide their teams effectively. Active listening is crucial for effective communication. It involves tuning in to what the speaker is saying, understanding their message, and responding appropriately. It's not just about hearing the words, but also picking up on nonverbal cues.

When a leader practices active listening, they can address any issues, provide support, and build trust within their team. Nonverbal communication, like body language, plays a big role in this too. Things like hand gestures, eye contact, and posture can show confidence, openness, and trustworthiness.

To drive your point home, make sure your body language matches what you're saying. Keep eye contact, nod along, and use open body language to make your interactions more effective. So, next time you're chatting with someone, pay attention to not only what they're saying, but how they're saying it.

Being specific and concise is super important for effective communication. Managers and supervisors need to communicate clearly so everyone understands. Avoiding jargon makes it easier for everyone to get the message. Good communication reduces misunderstandings and helps people feel confident in their roles.

Empathy is key too. Understanding where someone else is coming from helps build connections. An empathetic leader can resolve conflicts and be a supportive listener. This emotional bond creates a positive work environment that values teamwork.

Feedback is crucial for growth. Positive, detailed feedback helps people improve reasonably. It's important to highlight areas for improvement while still showing appreciation and motivation. Regular feedback sessions keep communication flowing and encourage development and accountability. Flexibility in the communication process is also vital and needed. It is quite obvious that a particular case or person may need various actions. It is known that a good leader always tries to evaluate the necessities of the team and reorganize their interactions. This may require the manager to be more assertive in times of emergency more consultative during planning crises, and more empathetic during staff personal problems. The use of narratives is one of the best strategies that can be employed when it comes to the dissemination of messages and passing on proper moral standards. People may find it easier to relate or to relate with something that has been narrated for example through success stories and personal stories. We find out that narratives in the culture can portray snapshots of the larger picture, the major message, and/or the call to action. Stories are one of the most powerful tools in the communication process as they always touch people's hearts and have profound effects. One more kind of activity is to ask questions that can be answered by describing something in detail for instance. This fosters discussion and calls on the members of the team to contribute their views. This way open-ended questions show that the leader is listening and encourages creativity and contribution from his team. Continuity of the messages makes a difference since they create trust. Thus, effective communication fosters stability and clarity of expectation among the employees or subordinates. Repetition of these messages increases trust and guarantees that all the people understand the organizational goals and objectives that it has set. That is why in the modern world is crucial to use technology for the amplification of communication. Technology-enabled communication tools such as video conferencing, instant messaging and collaborative platforms will enhance information exchange in real time. It too calls for efficient use of the digital mode of communication while at the same time embracing the use of a face-to-face mode of communication to establish an intimate touch. Interpersonal skills are very complex since they involve the ability to able to communicate effectively for some time continually. These are the techniques that can enable the leader to effectively engage and manage the subordinates in a manner that fosters the success of the group through understanding the team members, as well as motivating them hence achieving the organizational goals.

Conflict Resolution

There was some kind of tension, people had resentments and unresolved anger and frustrated feelings on both sides of the boardroom table. All the executives around the table wore looks of business-like and calm but everyone was as mad as hell. Similar scenes are often observed in the struggle for power in large companies where conflicting concepts, massive goals, and the executive's pride are not rare. It is important to highlight that conflict is inevitable in any organization and this calls for effective conflict resolution skills from any leader particularly the one who leads with qualities of heart. It is not just about how to refrain from voicing out negative sentiments or how to cover up an offended feeling. It's all about creating a culture that encourages open dialogue and values every opinion in an organization. Conflict is seen as an opportunity for growth, rather than a problem. Let's make sure everyone's voice is heard and respected.

Before a fight breaks out and a leader can make progress, it's important to establish a sense of understanding and connection with everyone involved. This involves taking the time to see things from their point of view and listening to what they're trying to communicate. It's also crucial to pay attention to body language and tone of voice, as they can often convey more than words alone.

Integrity plays a key role in resolving conflicts. A leader should be honest and open, willing to address serious issues head-on and not shy away from problems. This includes owning up to mistakes, both personally and as a team, and being open to feedback. Setting a good example is important, as it helps create a culture of accountability and problem-solving within the group.

By building empathy and maintaining integrity, a leader can prevent many issues from escalating and foster a positive and productive environment for everyone involved.

Effective communication is key in resolving conflicts. It's important to foster teamwork and cooperation among team members. Research suggests that team members should work together to find solutions that benefit everyone involved. This shifts the focus from conflict to collaboration, turning a potential battle into a project. It may take time and effort to have difficult conversations, but it's necessary for progress. When a leader emphasizes goals and values, employees will shift their focus from disagreements to group performance.

Another important aspect of conflict resolution is the strategic component. A key part of being a good leader is being able to see beyond the surface of a conflict and identify the underlying issues. Most conflicts are not as simple as they may appear at first glance. This may involve delving into aspects of organizational behaviour, examining hierarchies, or analysing interpersonal dynamics within a team. Once the root causes of a conflict have been identified, a leader can implement systems and policies to prevent similar issues from arising in the future, such as through training and development activities.

In addition, emotional intelligence plays a crucial role in the conflict resolution process. A leader must demonstrate emotional intelligence throughout the process by remaining calm and composed, even in the face of strong emotions. It is important to maintain composure regardless of how you may be feeling. This demonstrates that conflicts are a natural part of workplace dynamics, but they can be handled with professionalism and respect.

Conflict resolution involves building trust among team members. When team members believe that their leader genuinely cares about them and treats them fairly, they will respond with honesty and integrity. This trust is crucial for creating a cohesive and effective team that can effectively address challenges in the workplace.

Leading with empathy not only helps to understand conflicts on a deeper level but also fosters unity within the team. It creates a sense of belonging, where every team member feels valued and essential, like a part of a close-knit family.

Empowering Team Members

Empowerment goes beyond just being a trendy management term - it's a powerful process that breathes life into a team by making its members feel valued and capable. A strong team is built on the belief that each person has unique talents to offer. When managers and leaders embrace this belief, they create a culture of delegation and ownership among their teams, motivating them to perform at their best. During our interviews, one of the women we spoke with really nailed the idea of having empowered team members. She said, "Trust is one of the biggest factors in creating empowered team members." Empowerment is all about trust because it's seen as the key element. When leaders trust their team, it shows that they have high expectations for them. It's not just blind trust, though. It's a realistic trust where everyone's strengths, weaknesses, work experience, and goals are taken into account. Good leaders make sure to spend quality time with their team to understand what they're capable of. This helps them assign tasks more efficiently by matching them with the right people who can handle them best. Clear communication is the other none negotiable tool that needs to be implemented while empowering the team. Certainly, formal leaders must present clear responsibility and expectations and show the subordinates where they stand in a specific project and what role they play. Therefore, communication keeps on being an open channel through which the giving or receiving of feedback is established. This type of dialogue does create a sense of responsibility within the team since employees feel that their opinions are being considered in the process. It is crucial to ensure that every individual has the opportunity to enhance their career advancement. Leaders who support their subordinates' professional development prove that they care about the member's well-being and career. This may come in many shapes ranging from a more standardized approach in professional training courses to mentoring and learning by other experiences on the job. In this way, leaders prepare their team members and give them all the necessary tools, which in turn results in team members being ready to undertake new projects.

Recognition and appreciation also play vital roles in empowerment. Acknowledging individual and collective achievements boosts morale and reinforces positive behaviour. Leaders should celebrate both small wins and significant milestones, making sure to highlight the contributions of each team member. This recognition not only motivates individuals but also fosters a sense of companionship and collective pride within the team.

Empowerment is not about surrendering control but about creating a balanced dynamic where leadership and autonomy coexist. Leaders set the direction and provide the necessary resources and support, while team members take ownership of their tasks and decisions. This balance encourages innovation, as team members feel free to explore new ideas and approaches without fear of failure. Leaders should create a safe environment where mistakes are viewed as learning opportunities rather than setbacks.

Ultimately, empowering team members is about fostering a culture of trust, communication, growth, and recognition. It requires leaders to be intentional in their actions and consistent in their support. When team members feel empowered, they are more engaged, motivated, and committed to their work. They become more than just employees; they become partners in the journey towards achieving shared goals. Through empowerment, leaders unlock the full potential of their team, driving success and creating a workplace where everyone thrives.

Fostering Innovation

In today's leadership landscape, fostering innovation is crucial to grow and succeed as an organisation. The book "Leading with Heart" examines how to ignite creativity and embrace new thinking. It demonstrates how compassionate leadership can influence innovation.

Innovation begins when you create an environment where every person feels valued and has the freedom to voice their perspectives. Leaders who prioritize empathy and support for others establish an atmosphere where people don't fear speaking up even if their ideas seem unusual. This friendly approach opens the door for a wide range of creative ideas to come together and create innovative solutions.

Listening is essential for generating new ideas. When bosses take the time to listen to their team's thoughts and concerns, it shows that they care and respect their employees. This helps build trust and promotes the sharing of ideas. When team members feel valued, they are more willing to take risks and share new suggestions, knowing that their contributions are appreciated by others.

Creating space to experiment is also crucial. Effective leaders understand that mistakes are part of innovation. By viewing failures as learning opportunities rather than errors, leaders encourage their teams to try new things without fear. This helps people recover and improve driving the organisation towards major innovations.

Also, recognizing and celebrating creativity influences encouraging fresh ideas. When bosses applaud and reward innovative efforts regardless of their outcome, they demonstrate that creativity is valued in the organisation. Cheering for small wins and creative milestones boosts morale and motivates team members to persist with their groundbreaking projects.

Teamwork plays a crucial role in sparking new ideas. Great leaders remove barriers and promote collaboration among teams from different departments. They recognize that the best ideas come from individuals with different skills and perspectives working together. By facilitating collaboration, leaders create an environment where innovation can thrive. This leads to impressive results as people combine their strengths and build on each other's ideas.

Investing in continuous education and development has an impact on innovation. Leaders who prioritize their team's growth provide access to fresh knowledge, abilities, and opportunities. This enables team members to think and stay current in their field. This investment doesn't just improve individual job performance - it also drives the entire organisation's capacity to innovate.

Leading with empathy demonstrates that new ideas stem from collective effort under supportive leadership, not from a single person. When managers foster a workplace where everyone feels included listened to secure to experiment, valued able to collaborate, and learn fresh ideas emerge.

This approach has an impact on more than just the organisation's current situation. When employees have the freedom to innovate and work under caring supportive leaders, they become more engaged in their tasks, feel more motivated, and buy into the organisation's vision. The alignment of personal goals with organizational objectives drives the entire group toward long-term success and a track record of innovation.

"Leading with Heart" demonstrates how compassion, respect, and a desire to enhance each individual's creative abilities can foster innovation.

When leaders genuinely care, generating new ideas becomes more than just a result - it becomes a fundamental aspect of the organization's operations, driving continuous improvement over time.

Chapter - 4
Cultivating a Positive Work Culture

Trust and Transparency

When it comes to being a great leader, trust and transparency are like the dynamic duo. Trust is the foundation of any successful organization - you can't just turn it on and off when it's convenient. It's a crucial part of effective leadership that you have to work on earning every single day through your words and actions.

Transparency is like the trusty sidekick that helps support and strengthen the trust you've built. It means being open and honest about what you're doing and why you're doing it. People deserve to know what's going on behind the scenes when decisions are being made.

A leader who prioritizes trust and transparency knows that it's not just about sharing information, but also about building relationships. It's about being approachable, showing vulnerability, and admitting that you don't have all the answers. This kind of humility and openness creates a safe space for team members to speak up without fear of backlash. This leads to a more united and innovative team, where different perspectives are welcomed and appreciated.

In any organization, trust and transparency play a huge role in how things run smoothly. It's important to have open lines of communication, like regular town hall meetings and clear performance goals, so everyone knows what's expected of them. Leaders should be honest about both their successes and failures, showing that they're always learning and growing.

Being dependable and consistent is also key to building trust. If a leader says they'll do something, they should follow through. If things change and they can't keep their promise, they need to be upfront about why and come up with a new plan. Consistency like this is what builds a reputation for reliability, which is crucial for long-term trust.

The ripple effect of trust and transparency extended beyond the team and influenced the overall culture of the organization. This positive influence often spills over into the organization's reputation with clients, partners, and other stakeholders. People are more likely to want to work with those who prioritize integrity and transparency. As a result, this leads to stronger partnerships, increased loyalty, and a competitive edge in the market.

Building trust and transparency takes effort, no doubt about it. It means being aware of the work involved and being willing to confront some uncomfortable truths. It's a delicate balancing act for leaders - being open while also protecting sensitive information. This balance is key in deciding what to share and how to share it.

Leaders who can master this balancing act create an environment where people feel safe, appreciated, and motivated. They lay the groundwork for a strong, adaptable organization that can handle challenges and seize opportunities. In today's complex world of leadership, trust and transparency aren't just nice extras - they're essential qualities of effective and caring leadership.

Recognition and Appreciation

The morning sun's golden rays streamed through the office, filling the space with a sense of purpose and energy that inspired every employee. It was a place where ambition thrived, but so did camaraderie. In this lively setting, the leader wasn't just a boss, but a beacon of support and gratitude. The leader understood that recognizing and valuing each person's worth was crucial in helping them reach their full potential.

Recognition was first an art of observing the simple things: in nods at meetings, in smiles up and down the lobby, and in the "How was your weekend?" type questions. All these small gestures came together to create a sense of appreciation that communicated to every team member, "You are valued." The leader always made sure to be present, both physically and emotionally, to create an environment where everyone felt heard and valued.

Appreciation was always in the air, blending seamlessly with our daily tasks. It was the little notes left on our desks, recognizing our achievements big and small. Our leader's words were more than just compliments - they were heartfelt acknowledgements that touched our souls. "Your hard work on this project has truly made a difference," he would say, looking each of us in the eye.

This kind of recognition wasn't rare; it was part of our work culture. Appreciation didn't have to be fancy or formal; it thrived in our everyday interactions, building trust and respect.

Our leader made a point to highlight the strengths of each team member, especially when we were all together. By doing so, he spread that appreciation throughout the team, boosting morale. "Let's give a round of applause to Sarah for her creative approach to our latest challenge," he might say, prompting cheers and a sense of unity in the room.

What's more, the leader acknowledged that listening was a form of appreciation. They would ask open-ended questions in one-on-one meetings and listen so that employees could share everything from their thoughts and worries to hopes for the future. These discussions went beyond information exchange; they had to do with comprehending and therefore validating the unique contributions of each team member. It means that after hearing his employee out, a good leader would sum up, "I hear you, and your input is invaluable," thus making the employee walk out with renewed sense and purpose.

In this supportive environment, mistakes were not met with harsh criticism but with helpful feedback. The leader viewed errors as opportunities for growth and praised effort and intention. They would say, "I admire your willingness to take risks. Let's see what we can learn from this." This mindset created a culture where people were not afraid to fail but instead focused on constantly improving.

As time progressed, all these effects of the leadership style became even more evident. Employees were more engaged, creativity was at an all-time high, and overall, a sense of great loyalty seemed to emerge. The workplace was like a close-knit community, where giving recognition and showing appreciation were not just actions, but also guiding principles for how we interacted with each other.

It is with such an atmosphere of flourishing that the leader's commitment to recognizing and appreciating their members laid the very foundation of their success. It showed what true appreciation can do: changing the ordinary into something much more and binding people with different backgrounds into one cohesive, motivated, and energized team.

Work-Life Balance

The rhythm of a leader's life is like a symphony of never-ending demands, where the line between work and personal life blurs into a complex, sometimes chaotic harmony. Finding balance in this delicate ball can feel like chasing a horizon that keeps moving further away. But at the heart of it all is the essence of leading with compassion.

Balancing meetings, deadlines, and tough decisions requires careful planning and ultimately leads to achieving work-life balance. This balance is a reflection of how well someone can navigate the various roles thrust upon them as a leader. It's not just about managing time; it's about cultivating an attitude where professional goals and personal fulfilment are given equal importance. This equilibrium fosters resilience, sparks creativity, and keeps the fire of energy burning bright - a crucial element for effective leadership.

Imagine a leader who starts each day with a mindfulness practice - maybe some quiet time in the morning or a refreshing walk in the wet grass. These small acts of self-care serve as an anchor, grounding them in the present moment and preparing them to tackle the day's challenges with clarity and purpose. At work, they approach every task with focus, understanding that their well-being directly impacts their ability to inspire and guide their team.

In this sensitive balance, boundaries play an enormously important role. Set limits on their work instinctive understanding to set them by the leader-reclaim precious time for personal passions and family connections. The nature of such boundaries is not one of barriers but bridges, facilitating easy movement from the professional into the personal. They enable the leader to be fully present, whether it is during a boardroom discussion or dinner with the family, each experience enriched by undivided attention and engagement.

The heart-led leader knows delegation and trust. By empowering his people to take ownership of projects and decisions, he builds a collaborative atmosphere where people can flourish and be inventive. The leader frees himself from the suffocating weight of micromanagement. This is a two-way street: as the team gains in confidence and capability, so, too, the leader has more space to follow his interests and recharge his energies.

Another important pillar underpinning the balance is being able to make time in daily life for moments of pleasure and rest. Be that hobbies, sports, or simple quality time with loved ones, these activities recharge one's batteries and neutralize the heavy burden of leadership intensity. They remind us that life with all its light doesn't stop with or inside the office walls.

The heart-based approach toward leadership sees how the well-being of one reflects the others in the organization. Through modelling balanced living, leaders set a great example for the team, showing a way of being in which personal health and professional excellence are not mutually exclusive. Perhaps this may be part of the culture in which talent is attracted and retained and a better way for people to feel valued, supported, effective, and innovative.

In such pursuit of work-life balance, the heart-led leader continues to agree to his inner compass, always readjusting to keep in balance. This continuous process requires self-awareness, adaptability, and personal growth. It is about continuous learning and making courageous choices honoring professional ambitions and personal values.

As pioneers navigate this confusing and complex territory, they come to understand that real balance is not a point of relaxation but a moving equilibrium that can adjust when the situation changes. In this perspective, work-life balance not only remains a dream but becomes a way of life, a method of leadership in which every move is led by the heart with elegance and sagacity.

Inclusive Practices

It's about creating a working environment where all individuals feel valued and included. Such leaders foster a sense of belonging beyond the boundaries, purporting that diverse voices are heard and valued. They also recognize that having a variety of perspectives, backgrounds, and experiences contributes to the overall success of their teams. This diversity is key to driving innovation and fostering growth within organizations.

An inclusive leader needs to create a work environment that celebrates differences rather than just tolerating them. This requires a deep commitment to understanding the unique perspectives and experiences that each team member brings to the table. Inclusive leaders actively seek to learn about the cultural, social, and personal backgrounds that shape their colleagues' thinking. By doing so, they build trust and respect, which allows for open communication and true collaboration to thrive.

Treating everyone fairly is crucial for creating an inclusive environment. It means giving everyone the same chances to succeed and be recognized. Leaders need to make sure they are always looking out for any obstacles that might be holding back certain groups. This could involve changing how we hire people, setting up mentorship programs, and making sure there are clear paths for career growth for everyone.

Communication is very important to foster inclusive practices. It means that leaders have to develop skills in conversational approaches which allow them not only to attend to the complexity of diversity but also create ways for others to tell their story and bring valuable insight into the discussion. It's about creating safe spaces where people feel free to be themselves; this is how leaders can discover hidden talent and build mutual respect.

Good leaders don't just talk the talk, they walk the walk. They show a real interest in what others have to say and aren't afraid to challenge their assumptions and biases. This kind of self-awareness creates an environment where everyone can keep learning and growing.

When leaders are open about their journey towards inclusivity, it inspires their team to do the same. Inclusive practices don't just benefit the team, they have a positive impact on the whole organization and community. By leading the way in inclusivity, leaders encourage others to follow suit, creating a ripple effect that can change the entire organizational culture.

To make sure inclusivity sticks around, leaders need to make it a part of the organization's core values and practices. This way, inclusivity becomes a natural and lasting part of the workplace.

The effectiveness of the practice of inclusion should be measured with metrics and feedback mechanisms. Leaders should listen to constructive feedback and not be afraid to change course when necessary. That is, leaders continuously re-evaluate practices and make adjustments to keep their work of inclusivity relevant and effective.

Inclusive leadership thrives on acknowledging and celebrating human diversity. It's all about making sure every person feels seen, heard, and valued. Leaders who prioritize inclusivity in their practices not only boost the well-being and satisfaction of their teams but also drive innovation and success by embracing diverse perspectives. By intentionally focusing on equity and staying committed to creating an inclusive environment, leaders can pave the way for a brighter and more vibrant future for everyone.

Sustaining Morale

In every organization, morale is the pulse of the rhythm, which gives that organization the heartbeat to decide the level of collective energy and enthusiasm of its members. Leading from the heart is not just about navigating challenges, but also about fostering a sense of motivation and empowerment within others. Having high morale is like adding oil to the gears of innovation - it keeps things running smoothly, promotes teamwork, and creates a workplace where everyone feels appreciated and inspired.

There needs to be a leader first and foremost. Authenticity and transparency are cornerstones: when leaders are open about their victories and failures, they create a sense of trust. That's the bedrock on which morale will stand. Employees need to see their leaders as more than just figureheads. They should be active participants in the mission, sharing burdens and celebrating triumphs with their teams.

Recognition and appreciation are powerful catalysts to ensure morale is taken care of. Acknowledging any achievements, no matter how small, can boost morale and create a positive environment. Recognition should be timely and specific, highlighting not just the achievement but also the effort and hard work that was put in to achieve it. A heartfelt note, a public acclamation, or even a simple 'thank you' will do. By doing so, ripples of encouragement and motivation will take place.

Another critical path involves creating opportunities for growth and development. When team members can envision opportunities for growth in their professional and personal lives, it resonates with them. Leaders can foster this by providing access to training, mentoring, and new challenges that stretch abilities and build confidence. This will make the workforce more engaged and forward-looking with continuous learning and curiosity.

Besides that, it is equally important to be on top of work-life balance. Burnout is a silent killer of morale. Leaders must therefore be at guard to foster such practices that afford time for employees to reenergize and recover. This could be in the form of allowing flexibility in work schedules, providing resources on mental health, or simply encouraging them to take time off. For sure, when employees feel their well-being matters, commitment and morale will bloom naturally.

Communication is the key to keeping everything running smoothly. When we have open, honest, and frequent communication, it helps everyone on the team understand the vision and goals of the organization. Being able to have a two-way conversation allows for updates, feedback, and listening sessions where leaders and employees can share their thoughts and concerns. This dialogue not only helps avoid misunderstandings but also creates a sense of belonging and shared purpose.

Team cohesion is another important aspect of morale. It's all about how well your team works together and supports each other. When everyone is on the same page and has each other's backs, morale tends to be higher. So, make sure your team is cohesive and united to boost overall morale. There would be a feeling of good interpersonal relationships within the team, which could translate to better support for one another and a more cooperative atmosphere. Team-building activities formal and informal-served to create bonds between people that surpass the needs of getting the job done. Individuals feel connected with their co-workers and thus are bound to support each other to work in tandem towards the fulfilment of shared goals.

Leaders need to show adaptability and resilience as behaviors for their teams to emulate. Being able to navigate change with a positive outlook and problem-solving mindset can turn setbacks into opportunities for improvement. A culture that embraces challenges instead of fearing obstacles leads to steady morale during tough times.

In the world of leadership, keeping morale high is like the glue that holds everything together. It's all about finding the right balance of empathy, recognition, communication, and support. When a leader leads with compassion, it not only helps teams succeed but also creates a positive atmosphere where morale is high and everyone is motivated to do their best.

Chapter - 5

Emotional Intelligence in Leadership

Understanding Emotional Intelligence

Emotional intelligence, or EQ, is the ability to recognize, understand, and manage our own emotions, as well as being able to recognize, understand, and influence the feelings of others. This skill is essential in leadership because it impacts how leaders handle stress, make decisions, and communicate with their teams. While cognitive intelligence measures intellectual capacity, EQ goes further by exploring the complexities of human interaction and self-control.

Leadership skills consist of five key components: self-awareness, self-regulation, motivation, empathy, and social abilities. Self-awareness means being in tune with your true feelings, strengths, weaknesses, and how you affect others. It's about understanding yourself deeply, which helps you stay grounded and authentic as a leader. When leaders are self-aware, they handle criticism well and use it to improve themselves.

Self-regulation is all about being able to control your emotions and impulses, especially when things get tough. This is super important for leaders because it helps them stay calm under pressure, think before they act, and avoid making hasty decisions they might regret later. Leaders who are good at self-regulation can build trust and create a fair environment because they seem steady and reliable.

Motivation, as a part of emotional intelligence, goes beyond just wanting to achieve something; it involves having a genuine interest in reaching a goal with energy and determination. Leaders who are truly motivated not only strive for their success but also for the success of their team and organization. These managers are passionate about their work, resilient in the face of challenges, and have a strong desire to keep improving.

Empathy is the ability to understand and share the feelings of others. It helps leaders connect with their team on a deeper level, making team members feel valued and understood. Empathetic leaders can sense the emotions within their team, which is useful for resolving conflicts and building relationships. They can see things from others' perspectives, which improves communication and collaboration.

Social skills are the last piece of the emotional intelligence puzzle and involve managing relationships to guide people towards desired outcomes. This includes effective communication, conflict resolution, and the ability to inspire and motivate others. Leaders with strong social skills excel at building networks, managing teams, and creating a positive organizational culture. Socially adept leaders are often seen as charismatic and nice because they know how to bring out the best in their team.

Emotional intelligence is not set in stone; it's all about developing skills that can be improved over time. When leaders focus on boosting their EQ, they can anticipate seeing enhancements in their leadership abilities, team interactions, and overall organizational success. By being more aware of and nurturing these aspects, leaders can create a more harmonious, efficient, and emotionally intelligent work environment.

Self-Regulation Techniques

Being an effective and sensitive leader means being able to manage yourself and your reactions that may come up along the way. Self-regulation techniques are key to staying calm, making smart decisions, and creating a positive environment for your team. It's not about ignoring negative emotions, but using them as a guide and channeling them in the right direction.

One of the simplest self-regulation techniques is mindfulness. This means being present in the moment, and aware of your thoughts, feelings, and surroundings without passing judgment. Practicing mindfulness helps you pause before reacting, so you can respond thoughtfully instead of impulsively. Regular mindfulness meditation can help improve emotional balance and decision-making skills.

Deep breathing exercises are another great way to regulate yourself. When you're feeling stressed or under pressure, deep breathing triggers your body's relaxation response. This helps reduce symptoms of stress like a racing heart and tense muscles, allowing you to stay calm and composed. Leaders can use deep breathing to stay centred and set a positive tone for their teams.

Other helpful methods for leaders to manage their emotions include cognitive reframing. This is when a leader changes their perception of a situation to change how they feel about it. For example, instead of seeing a difficult situation as a threat, they can view it as an opportunity for growth or learning. This can help reduce anxiety and make their approach to the situation more positive and proactive. While cognitive reframing takes practice and self-awareness, it can greatly improve a leader's performance.

Journaling is another useful tool for self-regulation. By writing about their experiences, leaders can gain insight into their emotional triggers and patterns. This can help them better manage their reactions in the future. Journaling also allows leaders to set goals, values, and intentions, reinforcing their commitment to lead with heart.

Physical activity is also important for self-regulation. Regular exercise not only benefits physical health but also mental well-being. Activities like running, yoga, or even a brisk walk can help release tension and stress, bringing about emotional balance. Leaders who prioritize physical activity often have the energy and focus to meet the demands of their role.

Practising gratitude is a great way for leaders to shift their mindset from stress and negativity to appreciation and positivity. By taking time to reflect on and acknowledge the things they are grateful for regularly, leaders can maintain a more optimistic outlook overall. This could be as simple as keeping a gratitude journal or taking a few moments each day to think about the positive aspects of life. Having a grateful attitude can help improve emotional resilience and create a more encouraging and inspiring environment for team members.

Connecting with colleagues, mentors, or coaches who understand the pressures of leadership is a key self-regulation strategy. Talking to others who can relate to the challenges of being a leader can provide valuable perspective and emotional support. This support network allows leaders to share their feelings, receive feedback, and explore different ways to handle difficult situations.

Incorporating these self-regulation techniques into daily life is a great way to start leading with heart. This practice not only benefits leaders themselves but also their teams by improving emotional intelligence, empathy, and resilience.

Motivation and Inspiration

The path of a leader is often guided by the powerful forces of motivation and inspiration. These two elements are not just abstract concepts but are deeply intertwined in the essence of successful leadership. They serve as the driving force that propels leaders forward and ignites the passions of those they lead.

In those quiet moments before the sun rises, when the world is still and thoughts are undisturbed, is when most leaders find their motivation. It is during these peaceful times that a leader can truly tap into their inner drive. Whether it's a personal mission, a vision for a better future, or a desire to make a lasting impact, motivation comes from deep within the soul. It acts as a guiding compass, ensuring that every action and decision is purposeful and aimed towards something greater.

Inspiration, on the other hand, can be found in the interactions and experiences that shape a leader's journey. It could be the story of a team member who overcame incredible odds, the wise words of a mentor, or the energy of a group working together towards a common goal. Inspiration is the external force that brings a leader's vision to life, transforming it from a mere dream into a tangible reality. It is the gentle nudge towards pushing boundaries and exploring new territories.

Motivation and inspiration together create a dynamic synergy that amplifies a leader's effectiveness. Where motivation provides the steadfast determination to push through the challenges, inspiration offers creativity and enthusiasm for the pursuit. Combined, they make for a formidable team that, together, can tackle most obstacles and adjust to change before inspiring others to engage in pursuit.

A leader who leads with the heart knows that growth in motivation and inspiration goes hand in hand when it comes to driving activities within his team. To him, each has different reasons why he is motivated or inspired by a particular experience. He will therefore make sure each person is valued and empowered once these personal drivers are learned. This in turn builds a culture of mutual respect and cooperation whereby every team member gives his or her best and aspires for excellence.

Storytelling is only one powerful tool in the hands of a particular kind of leader. By sharing his experiences and what he has learned along the way, the leader may connect with his team on a deeper level. These stories serve as testimony to motivation and inspiration, showing how they have aligned the journey of a leader and can similarly do so for others. A leader can stir up a sense of purpose and passion in his or her team through stories and build a collective narrative that might tie them all together.

Motivation and inspiration in leadership are not fleeting, but enduring forces. They are the driving force behind a leader's mission, guiding their actions and resonating with those they lead. By nurturing these qualities within themselves and their team, a leader can make a lasting impact and go beyond the expectations of their role. Leading with passion allows a leader to turn their beliefs into actions and bring life to every endeavour.

Empathy in Action

The conference room was buzzing with excitement as everyone waited for the meeting to start. The chairs were arranged in a circle, creating a welcoming and inclusive atmosphere. At nine o'clock, Sarah, the team leader, walked in with a stack of notepads and a warm smile. She greeted each team member by name, showing genuine interest in their well-being.

Sarah had a unique leadership style that focused on building relationships with her team. She believed in the power of empathy and saw it as a crucial aspect of leadership. Today's meeting wasn't about numbers or deadlines; it was a chance for everyone to connect and share.

To kick things off, Sarah shared a personal story about a time when she felt overwhelmed and unsupported in her career. Her voice was steady, but there was a vulnerability that resonated with the team. It wasn't a rehearsed speech, but a genuine recount of her struggles. As she spoke, the room fell silent, with everyone captivated by her authenticity.

After finishing her part, she let others take the floor to share. Team members talked about their challenges, one after the other, some personal and some professional. There was John, who was balancing work with caring for his elderly parents, and Maria, who felt isolated working from home. Each story was different, but they all had one thing in common: they were fighting battles that many didn't know about.

Sarah listened intently, showing openness and compassion through her body language. She didn't interrupt or rush to provide solutions; she simply listened. The act of truly listening and hearing what others had to say was a powerful display of empathy in action. It created a safe space for people to express themselves without fear of judgment.

As the meeting progressed, Sarah began offering solutions to the issues raised. Instead of quick fixes, she posed thought-provoking questions and suggestions. She encouraged team members to work together to come up with solutions, fostering a sense of mutual responsibility and support. She helped John by offering a more flexible schedule and connecting him with resources for elder care. Maria suggested having virtual coffee meetings more frequently to combat feelings of isolation and urged the team to be more proactive in reaching out.

By the end of the meeting, there was a noticeable shift in the room's atmosphere. Tension had given way to camaraderie and understanding. Team members left with more than just action items; they left with a shared bond and emotional support.

Sarah's approach exemplified the incredible impact empathy can have on leadership. It's not just about understanding emotions, but about taking meaningful action based on that understanding. This human connection transformed the team dynamic into a culture of trust and collaboration.

In the following days, the effects of that meeting were still being felt. Productivity increased, but more importantly, team members felt valued and more comfortable. Sarah's empathetic leadership had a ripple effect, inspiring others to lead with their hearts as well. By simply listening and responding with compassion, what started as a routine meeting turned into a life-changing experience, highlighting the profound power of empathy in action.

Social Skills Development

The key to being a great leader is all about connecting with people on a deeper level. Developing strong social skills is crucial for those who want to lead with compassion and understanding. These skills help create a cohesive and motivated team where everyone feels valued and heard.

Communication is at the core of social skills development. Effective leaders can convey their ideas and listen to their team members. They can pick up on subtle cues and understand what others are trying to say. This intuitive understanding allows them to navigate social situations with ease and grace.

Empathy is another essential aspect of social skills for leaders. It goes beyond just understanding different perspectives - it's about genuinely caring for the well-being of others. Empathetic leaders can sense when someone on their team is struggling and can offer support in a way that makes people feel comfortable opening up.

Conflict resolution is also a key component of social skill development. Instead of seeing disagreements as obstacles, great leaders view them as opportunities for growth. They facilitate open and honest discussions, ensuring that all parties are heard and working towards mutually beneficial solutions.

Overall, honing social skills is essential for effective leadership. By connecting with others on a meaningful level, leaders can create a positive and productive work environment where everyone feels supported and valued.

It also involves the art of rapport-building. A leader who would take time to understand the strengths, weaknesses, and motivational factors of each of his team members could adapt his approach to fit the growth of that particular person's needs. This personalized attention to the needs of each of his team members not only enables high performance but also creates a sense of belonging and loyalty in them. Leaders reinforce a positive and inclusive culture by celebrating success and providing constructive feedback.

Adaptability is the hallmark of effective social skills. Any leader should know how to switch on or off certain aspects of his personality, depending on his audience and the situation. For this reason, he will be flexible enough to make quite sure that his message gets across and is crystal clear to an audience of very diversified orientations. Whether speaking in front of a large crowd or having a one-on-one chat, effective leaders can connect with others on a personal level and inspire them. They tune into the other person's frequency to truly engage and motivate them.

Non-verbal communication also plays a huge role. A conscious leader with positive body language, facial expressions, and tone of voice speaks volumes about his confidence and sincerity without saying a word. Minor telltales often convey more than verbal communication alone. They reinforce a message and enhance your credibility.

It is a constant development process of social skills through self-reflection and learning from experiences. In the process of continuous skill building, leaders will be improving more than anything else: increasing the collective potential among the team members. While doing so, they are developing a compassionate and, at the same time, very strong leadership style, managing their teams from the heart to create long-lasting success.

Chapter - 6
Building Trust with Your Team

The Role of Integrity

Integrity is often seen as the foundation of good leadership. It goes beyond just being honest and following moral rules. It means actually living out your values and principles, and making sure your actions match your words. In leadership, integrity isn't just a nice-to-have quality - it's a must-have. It's what builds trust and respect between leaders and their followers.

Imagine having a leader who always does the right thing. He's the type of person who doesn't freak out when things get tough or give in to shady deals just to make a quick buck. Instead, he stays true to his values, following his moral compass without hesitation. This kind of leader earns the trust of his team because they know he's fair and won't throw anyone under the bus.

Integrity doesn't just stop with the leader - it becomes part of the organization's DNA. It shapes how decisions are made and how people interact with each other. A leader who values integrity creates a team where communication flows freely, and everyone feels comfortable sharing their thoughts and concerns without fear of backlash. This open dialogue not only leads to better decisions but also fosters a strong sense of community.

When a leader leads with integrity, it motivates others to do the same. It creates a domino effect where following the rules becomes the norm. Team members take ownership of their work, hold themselves accountable, and strive for excellence because that's what the leader values and rewards.

There are lots of challenges to exercising integrity in leadership. Often, there can be pressure for performance targets, the satisfaction of stakeholders, or politically complicated environments. It is hard in such situations not to take shortcuts or find ways around compromising a decision or action. In the long run, any possible gains by such means are outweighed by the fact that credibility and loss of follower trust are seriously damaged.

Integrity is super important when it comes to handling a crisis. When things get tough, people look to their leaders for guidance and support. A leader who sticks to their principles during hard times is like a rock for their team. Being consistent and making decisions with integrity creates a sense of stability and trust within a group.

Integrity is the foundation of good leadership. It boosts a leader's credibility, builds trust, and creates a positive work environment. Without integrity, other leadership qualities like vision, empathy, and resilience won't have much impact because trust and respect are missing. So, if you want to be a great leader, you gotta have integrity - it's non-negotiable.

Integrity is like the beat that keeps everything in sync in the dance of leadership. It's the quiet thread that runs through every decision, action, and interaction, connecting leaders to themselves and their teams. You can't underestimate the importance of integrity in leadership; it's what makes leading with heart meaningful.

Consistency and Reliability

In the intricate dance of leadership, being consistent and reliable is crucial for building trust. These qualities act as strong pillars that shape a leader's character and define an organization's culture. They are not just about staying the course but embodying a set of guiding principles that others can rely on day in and day out.

Think of a lighthouse standing tall against crashing waves during a storm. It remains steadfast, never losing its light, providing comfort and direction to those navigating rough waters. Similarly, a steady and dependable leader serves as a beacon of strength for their team. People turn to this type of leader for guidance, knowing they can trust in their stability and reliability.

Consistency in leadership goes beyond following rules and procedures; it also means being predictable in actions and responses. When team members know what to expect, it reduces uncertainty and anxiety. This predictability creates a work environment where people feel safe to share ideas, innovate, and take risks. The leader's consistent behaviour sets a standard that permeates through the organization, fostering a culture where everyone understands expectations and strives to meet them, knowing their efforts will be recognized and rewarded fairly.

Being reliable means being someone others can always count on. It's all about keeping your word and following through on your promises. A reliable leader is someone who not only talks the talk but walks the walk, consistently delivering results. This trait is crucial for earning respect and building credibility with your team.

When a leader proves themselves to be reliable, it sends a clear message that they value others' time and efforts. This fosters mutual respect and accountability among team members. These qualities require self-awareness and a deliberate effort on the part of the leader. It's important to understand your values and make decisions that align with them consistently, even when faced with challenges and pressures.

Integrity is closely tied to consistency and reliability. These qualities are key indicators of a good leader with strong moral and ethical standards. By embodying integrity, consistency, and reliability, a leader can enhance their credibility and increase their influence and inspiration.

In essence, integrity, consistency, and reliability are the building blocks of effective leadership. By embodying these traits, a leader can earn the trust and respect of their team, ultimately leading to greater success and cohesion within the group.

In simple terms, being transparent, setting clear expectations, and taking responsibility for your actions is key to effective communication. This means acknowledging and fixing any discrepancies between what you say and what you do. To gain trust and be reliable, leaders need to own up to their mistakes and make things right.

When leaders consistently show they are trustworthy and reliable, their team will be loyal and dedicated. This creates a strong, united group that can achieve amazing things. Building trust and respect through consistent and reliable leadership not only improves performance but also creates a positive work environment.

Open Communication

In any team or organization, the vibe is all about how well everyone communicates. Leaders who are all about open communication create an environment where trust, innovation, and personal growth can thrive. It's not just about having an open-door policy - it's about truly listening, understanding, and responding to what everyone has to say.

Picture this: a leader whose office is like a safe space for chatting. It's bright, cosy, and welcoming, just like the leader. People feel comfortable sharing their thoughts because they know they'll be heard and respected. This leader knows that every voice matters, and sometimes the best ideas come from unexpected places. By creating an environment where people can be themselves, the leader encourages creativity and teamwork.

During meetings, this leader doesn't hog the spotlight. Instead, they guide the conversation by asking thoughtful questions and encouraging team members to speak up. When someone shares an idea, the leader listens carefully, nods, and gives feedback to show they appreciate the input. This approach empowers team members and makes them feel like they have a stake in the team's success.

This leader is open and honest in their communication. They talk about both wins and losses, demystifying the decision-making process. If things aren't going well, the leader doesn't shy away from discussing it. Instead, they bring the team together to brainstorm solutions. This builds trust and turns problems into opportunities for collaboration.

The leader also sends messages without speaking: he maintains eye contact, smiles reassuringly, and keeps his body language open. These subtle cues confirm that he is approachable and caring. By being aware of his body language, the manager ensures that his actions match his words.

In addition to promoting open communication within the team, the leader also encourages dialogue between different departments. They organize regular meetings and social events that bring people from different areas together, breaking down barriers and fostering a sense of unity. These interactions often lead to unexpected collaborations and innovative solutions as diverse perspectives are shared.

At the core of this communication strategy is technology. The leader utilizes various tools to keep communication channels open, such as newsletters, virtual town halls, and collaborative platforms where team members can share ideas and feedback in real-time. By embracing these tools, the leader ensures that communication is not limited by physical boundaries, allowing for a more robust exchange of ideas.

This leader views communication as more than just sharing information - it's about building a community. They understand that without respect and understanding among team members, true success is unattainable. By promoting open communication, the leader makes individuals feel valued and heard, setting the stage for a successful, cohesive, and creative team.

Respecting Boundaries

One key aspect to consider is the importance of professional boundaries. Compassionate leaders who lead with heart understand that maintaining boundaries is not just a formality, but a way to show respect for their team members' personal space, time, and emotions. By respecting these boundaries, leaders create a safe and valued environment where trust and loyalty can thrive.

A boundary-aware leader knows how to balance accessibility with professionalism. They don't pry into personal matters unless invited to do so, showing sensitivity and respect for their team's privacy. When employees feel that their personal lives are respected, they are more likely to be engaged and productive at work.

Respecting boundaries also extends to communication. Sending emails late at night or expecting immediate responses on weekends can intrude on employees' time. Setting clear expectations for communication, such as only accepting work messages during certain hours, shows respect for personal time and helps prevent burnout.

Physical boundaries in the workplace are also important. Just because there's an open-door policy doesn't mean there isn't personal space for employees. It's crucial to create a space where employees can work in peace when they don't want to be disturbed, setting ground rules and fostering a respectful work environment.

Managing emotional boundaries can be quite challenging for leaders. It's important to be aware of your team's feelings without overstepping. This means knowing when someone needs help and offering support sensitively and appropriately. For instance, if an employee is going through a tough time, a compassionate leader might offer flexible scheduling or resources for professional assistance without prying into personal matters.

During meetings and team discussions, leaders must give everyone a chance to speak up and make sure their opinions are not only heard but also respected. Taking over conversations or dismissing ideas from team members creates a negative environment of exclusion and disrespect. By fostering a culture where people feel comfortable sharing their thoughts without fear of judgment, leaders can create a more inclusive and respectful workplace.

Respecting boundaries also involves recognizing the limits of your leadership role. It's important to understand that not every problem needs to be solved by the leader, and not every need can be met by them. Leaders should empower team members to take ownership of their work and lives and encourage them to seek help when needed. This promotes autonomy, self-reliance, and mutual support within the team.

When leaders set an example by respecting boundaries, it encourage others to do the same. This creates a ripple effect within organizations, leading to greater respect, consideration, and overall effectiveness in the workplace. By prioritizing the respect of boundaries, leaders can create an environment where everyone feels valued and empowered to contribute their best.

Repairing Trust After Missteps

When trust is broken, it can feel as delicate as a vase dropped on the floor and shattered into a thousand pieces. Mistakes are bound to happen in leadership, but it's how a leader handles those mistakes that shows the strength of their relationship with their team. When a leader messes up, it can shake the very foundation of trust within the organization.

The first step to rebuilding trust is owning up to the mistake. It takes a lot of courage for a leader to admit when they've messed up and come down to the same level as their team. Taking responsibility for the mistake sets a good example for accountability within the team. The leader needs to acknowledge the mistake without making excuses or blaming others.

After accepting the mistake, a sincere apology is necessary. A true apology goes beyond just saying "I'm sorry" - it shows genuine regret and a commitment to making things right. This helps the team see the leader as human and creates a sense of empathy among team members.

Actions speak louder than words when it comes to rebuilding trust. The leader needs to come up with a clear plan to fix the damage and prevent similar mistakes in the future. This plan should involve input from the team to ensure it's comprehensive and inclusive. By taking concrete steps to rectify the error, the leader not only empowers the team but also strengthens the bond between team members.

The key to all these steps is transparency. It's like a bridge of communication that keeps everyone in the loop and helps everyone understand the situation better. This helps get rid of any doubts and builds a culture of integrity and trust. Giving regular updates on progress, challenges, and changes also helps reassure the team that their leader is working to make things right.

Equally important is for the leader to follow through on their actions after making a mistake. Trust doesn't come back overnight; it takes time, patience, and a series of positive actions to earn it back. The leader needs to be reliable, stable, truthful, and genuinely care about their team. Consistency is key to rebuilding lost faith and showing that the mistake was a one-time thing.

During the recovery phase, empathy and patience are crucial. The leader needs to be aware of the emotional state of the team and understand that everyone heals at their own pace. By offering understanding and support, the leader creates a space for rebuilding confidence and trust.

Rebuilding trust after mistakes demonstrates a leader's dedication to their team, if done with honesty, empathy, and good intentions, strengthening the bond within the team.

Chapter - 7

Case Studies of Successful Servant Leaders

Corporate Leaders

In the tall skyscrapers of major corporations, where choices affect economies and plans shape industries, there are some special people: corporate leaders. These leaders aren't just your typical boardroom executives crunching numbers; they are the visionaries, the culture creators, and the driving force behind their organizations.

Amidst the constant buzz of computers and shuffling papers, these leaders stand out as beacons of inspiration. You can feel their presence as they confidently navigate through busy offices, seal important deals with firm handshakes, and carefully contemplate decisions that could change the lives of many. Each leader has a unique blend of charisma and authority, striking a balance between being approachable and commanding respect.

Their days are a whirlwind of meetings, strategy sessions, and impromptu chats with employees in the hallways. It is in these moments of authenticity that they truly shine. Corporate leaders are not just about giving orders; they are about fostering a collaborative and trusting environment where everyone's voice is heard.

So, next time you think of a corporate leader, remember that they are much more than just a title. They are the driving force behind the success of their organizations, leading with empathy, understanding, and a keen eye for what lies beneath the surface.

In the quiet of their offices, surrounded by trophies and memories of past victories, business leaders ponder what lies ahead. The weight of responsibility is always on their minds. They know that their choices impact not only the company's bottom line but also the lives of their employees and the communities they serve. This awareness shapes their leadership style, driving them to prioritize sustainable growth and ethical practices.

A leader's vision acts as a compass, guiding them through market ups and downs and technological changes. They resist the temptation of short-term gains, staying focused on long-term success. They communicate their goals clearly and passionately, inspiring their teams to work towards a common purpose. It is this shared vision that truly showcases their leadership strength, motivating others to believe in and strive for a future greater than the sum of its parts.

Outside the office, these leaders are influential figures. They attend industry conferences, where their presentations shape discussions on emerging trends and best practices. Their opinions are sought after by policymakers and thought leaders, and they are frequently interviewed by the media. Despite their external recognition, they remain grounded and connected to the people who contribute to their success.

What will set these business leaders apart in the end is not just their strategic skills or their ability to achieve results. They can lead with compassion. They understand that the key to a successful organization lies in building strong relationships based on trust, respect, and empathy. This understanding is what makes them true leaders, not only guiding their companies to success but also leaving a lasting impact beyond the business world.

Non-Profit Champions

The nonprofit world is pretty unique because leaders have to be both skilled and compassionate to handle all the challenges that come their way. These champions have a strong sense of purpose and are working hard to make real changes in the world. Nonprofit leadership is all about inspiring, mobilizing, and keeping up efforts that rely a lot on volunteers, donations, and community support.

But what sets successful nonprofit leaders apart is their unwavering dedication to their cause. Their passion is infectious and gets others excited to join in on the mission. When they talk about issues like homelessness, environmental sustainability, or education, they know exactly how to connect with people on a personal level. They tell stories that tug at the heartstrings and inspire a sense of shared responsibility among their supporters.

Empathy is a huge part of what makes nonprofit champions so effective. They just seem to understand the struggles and desires of the communities they're serving. This understanding helps them create programs that are not only successful but also culturally sensitive and relevant. By actively listening and engaging with stakeholders, they build trust and credibility - the foundation for making a lasting impact.

One key trait of successful nonprofit leaders is their resourcefulness. They have to work with limited budgets and resources, so they need to be able to make the most out of what they have. By forming partnerships, utilizing networks, and finding creative ways to secure funding, they can come up with cost-effective solutions that can be used in different situations.

Transparency and accountability are also crucial in nonprofit leadership. Leaders need to balance completing their missions with maintaining trust with donors, volunteers, and beneficiaries. This requires clear communication, detailed reporting, and ethical management of resources. By doing this, nonprofit organizations can keep their credibility intact and ensure their work is impactful.

Another important aspect of nonprofit leadership is managing and inspiring volunteers. Volunteers play a vital role in many nonprofits, bringing diverse skills and perspectives to the table. Effective leaders know how to motivate volunteers, making sure they feel appreciated and dedicated. By providing guidance, meaningful tasks, and growth opportunities, leaders can foster a sense of ownership and pride among their volunteers.

Adaptability is a crucial quality to have, especially in the nonprofit world. The landscape is always changing due to current policies, evolving funding sources, and emerging societal needs. Being able to quickly adjust to new challenges and opportunities is key for nonprofit leaders to stay relevant and achieve their goals.

Nonprofit champions also excel at building and nurturing relationships. They know that collaborating with others and engaging with the community can help expand the impact of their work. By forming partnerships with other organizations, government agencies, and private sector partners, they create a ripple effect that benefits everyone involved.

In the fast-paced world of nonprofits, leaders stand out not just for their dedication, but for leading with their hearts. Their resilience, compassion, and unwavering belief in the power of people coming together guide their journey. They light the way for others, showing that meaningful and lasting change is possible when passion meets purpose.

Community Organizers

Every successful community has dedicated community organizers working tirelessly behind the scenes. These individuals are the true heroes of grassroots movements, bringing people together and driving progress. Their job goes beyond just getting people involved - they also motivate, educate, and empower others. Whether in the busy city or peaceful countryside, community organizers are the driving force behind positive change, creating a space where shared goals can become reality.

Community organizing is all about connecting with the heartbeat of the people. Community organizers have a special talent for really listening to the concerns, hopes, and dreams of the people they serve. They spend their days walking the streets, attending local meetings, and having countless conversations to truly understand the unique challenges and strengths of their community.

Building trust is the key ingredient for a successful community organizer. It's not an easy task and often requires years of dedication and commitment. Trust is built through transparency, reliability, and genuine care for the well-being of the community. Organizers act as bridges between different groups, fostering communication and understanding where there was once only division. Their ability to bring together people from diverse backgrounds showcases their diplomatic skills and empathetic approach.

Education is another essential aspect of community organizing. Organizers simplify complex issues so that everyone can understand and work towards solutions. Workshops, seminars, and informal meetings provide opportunities for learning and growth. By breaking down barriers to information, organizers ensure that every community member has the tools to participate fully in the democratic process.

Mobilization is where the hard work of community organizers pays off. Whether it's organizing a protest, a cleanup, or any other event, mobilization is the tangible result of their efforts. These events require careful planning and the skill of rallying people towards a common goal. Organizers play a crucial role in bringing the community together to create positive change.

Community organizers have a lasting impact that goes beyond just the immediate results. The empowerment they instil in communities continues to grow long after a campaign or event is over. Effective organizing leads to a sense of agency and solidarity that sticks around. The memories and friendships formed during these efforts serve as the foundation for future collaboration and resilience.

At the core of community organizing is a belief in the power of collective action. Organizers strive for a world where everyone has the opportunity to thrive. It's not easy work - setbacks and obstacles are constant. But through it all, organizers remain resilient and optimistic. They are the ones who keep hope alive as they guide their communities through times of change.

Community organizers are the unsung heroes of social progress. They inspire and lead people towards a more just and equitable society. Their true leadership lies in empowering others to find their voice and take action. It's not about the power one holds, but about lifting others up to create real change.

Educational Pioneers

Throughout history, there have been some pretty awesome people who have changed the game when it comes to education. These trailblazers from the 19th and 20th centuries set the stage for how we learn today.

One of these education pioneers was John Dewey. He was all about pragmatism, which means learning through experience and reflection. Dewey thought that education should be based on real-life problems to get kids thinking for themselves. He was all about ditching the boring memorization and focusing on student-centred learning.

Thanks to Dewey, classrooms became more interactive and collaborative.

Then there's Maria Montessori, who had a whole different approach. She believed in giving kids independence and freedom within boundaries. Her specially designed materials and furniture created an environment where kids could explore and learn on their own. Montessori thought that the love for learning should start early and that education is a lifelong journey. Her influence can still be seen in classrooms worldwide, where her methods help students develop self-discipline and motivation.

However, Soviet psychologist Lev Vygotsky was all about the zone of proximal development - a super important concept that shows how cognitive development can happen through social interaction. Vygotsky's theories also pointed out that learning goes best when students are in cultural and social settings and have support from people who know more than them. This collaborative approach has led to a bunch of teaching strategies that focus on scaffolding and guided participation. The goal is to help learners reach their full potential with structured support.

Then there's Paulo Freire, a Brazilian educator and philosopher who shook things up in education. In his book Pedagogy of the Oppressed, Freire called out traditional education systems for keeping social inequalities alive and pushed for a more interactive problem-solving approach to learning. By pushing for critical thinking and empowerment, Freire wanted education to be a freeing experience where learners could take charge of their own freedom. His ideas have inspired tons of educators to adopt more inclusive and socially just teaching methods by challenging the status quo and pushing for fairness in education.

Some of the most influential figures in the special education field are Anne Sullivan and Jean Piaget. Anne Sullivan showed through her work with Helen Keller that miracles can happen when teachers are dedicated and caring. Jean Piaget's theories on cognitive development have helped educators understand how children learn and grow. His stages of development have guided teachers in adapting their teaching methods to meet the needs of their students.

These trailblazers have left a lasting impact on education, weaving together diverse ideas and practices that continue to inspire educators today. Their legacies remind us of the power of education and the importance of leading with compassion and foresight.

Healthcare Heroes

In the hustle and bustle of the hospital hallways and the quiet rooms of the clinics, some amazing people bring hope and comfort to those in need. These are the healthcare workers in their scrubs and lab coats, facing each new day with determination and dedication. They don't just see their job as a way to make a living, but as a true calling to help and heal.

In these medical sanctuaries, the air is filled with the smell of antiseptics and the tension of what's to come. But even in the midst of all that, there is a sense of compassion. Nurses, doctors, and support staff move with purpose and grace, their years of training and understanding of human vulnerability guiding them. To them, every patient is more than just a name on a chart or a list of symptoms - they are individuals with stories, fears, and dreams.

In the pediatric wing, the sound of machines beeping is interrupted by the laughter of children. A kind nurse captures their attention with a spontaneous puppet show, giving them a moment of distraction and joy. Her tired eyes light up with warmth as she adjusts an IV line with practiced skill, offering comfort to both the young patients and their worried parents.

Meanwhile, down the hall, a surgeon is getting ready for a complex operation. His hands are steady and confident, ready to perform life-saving procedures. The weight of the responsibility is heavy, but he carries it with a calm assurance that comes from years of experience in the operating room. His mind is a symphony of knowledge and skill, each decision a crucial note in the intricate process of healing the human body.

The atmosphere in the intensive care unit is pretty intense. Monitors beep in a steady rhythm as they monitor the balance of life. Critical care nurses are like guardians in this delicate thread of existence connected to eternity. They never stop watching over their patients, and their expertise shines bright in the darkness of uncertainty. They move gracefully through a sea of medical equipment, each touch of their hands a lifeline for those hanging on the edge.

Aside from taking care of their patients, these unsung heroes also offer support to their families. They lend a listening ear or words of encouragement, understanding that recovery is not just physical but also emotional and mental. Their ability to provide comfort during chaos shows their deep sense of empathy.

During quieter moments, when emergencies are on hold, these professionals can reflect on the lives they've impacted and the difference they've made. The victories may be small, but they are filled with gratitude. And even in the face of defeat, their determination remains strong as they continue their mission with renewed vigour.

These nurses are the heartbeat of every healthcare institution, and their dedication serves as a constant reminder of their nobility. They inspire not only their colleagues but also the communities they serve, leading with compassion and unwavering commitment. Their untold stories speak volumes about the incredible power of leading with heart.

Chapter - 8

Servant Leadership in Personal Life

Family Dynamics

In the cosy, sunlit kitchen of the Kumar's, the smell of freshly brewed coffee mixed perfectly with the scent of cinnamon rolls. The oak cabinets and checkered curtains gave off a comforting vibe like they were from a different time. This kitchen was the heart of the house, where laughter and serious talks happened every morning, showing the complex dynamics of the family.

Kumar, a man in his late forties, sat at the head of the table. He had a calm demeanour and thoughtful eyes that showed his years of experience and wisdom. He was the rock of the family - strong and stable. His leadership style was all about empathy and understanding. He believed in the power of listening and always made sure his children knew that their voices mattered.

Next to him was his wife Sunita, a lively woman with a nurturing spirit. Her contagious laughter and comforting hugs were just what the family needed on tough days. Sunita held the family together with her intuition and emotional intelligence. She could sense the unspoken emotions and guided the family with compassion through any rough patches.

Their teenage daughter, Rekha, sat across from them. She had a spark in her eyes that showed her curiosity and a touch of rebellion as she navigated through finding her identity and testing boundaries. Her passion for social justice led to lively debates at the dinner table, where she challenged her parents' views to carve out her path. Kumar and Sunita welcomed this, believing in raising their child to think critically and be independent.

Sunita's younger brother, Kiran, was a quiet kid who loved to draw. He had pieces of paper scattered all over the house, each one a window into his imagination. Despite his silence, Kiran wasn't disengaged; he was just a thoughtful observer of the world around him. His parents understood his need for space and solitude, supporting him in a way that honoured his unique personality.

The Kumar family had a special dynamic. Kumar and Sunita believed in leading with their hearts, creating an environment where everyone felt valued and heard. They held family meetings in their sunlit kitchen, using them as a way to communicate openly and strengthen their bond.

Of course, they faced challenges like any family. But disagreements were seen as opportunities for resolution, not conflict. Kumar's calm demeanour and Sunita's empathy were their guiding lights during tough times. They taught their children the importance of forgiveness and the power of vulnerability.

In the Kumar household, leadership wasn't about authority; it was about connection. Each family member's strengths and weaknesses were recognized and nurtured with love and patience. Kumar and Sunita led by example, showing their children that true leadership comes from caring for and respecting one another.

In their warm, bustling kitchen, the Kumar planted the seeds of compassionate leadership, ensuring a future where heart-centred approaches would guide their way.

Friendship and Social Circles

In the world of leadership, relationships are like the fuel that keeps us going. No leader can thrive without understanding the importance of friendships and social circles. These relationships aren't just a side note in the story of leadership; they are the main chapters that shape who we are as leaders. They provide us with support, challenges, and opportunities for growth.

Imagine a bustling marketplace filled with countless interactions. Each stall and pathway represents a different friendship or social circle, offering unique insights and experiences. A leader in this marketplace must be attuned to the subtleties of each connection, recognizing that every interaction presents a chance to make an impact on their leadership journey.

A great leader values diverse friendships because they bring a wealth of perspectives and ideas. These relationships span across various backgrounds and experiences, pushing a leader to think beyond their limitations. By surrounding themselves with people who think differently, a leader can broaden their horizons and gain a deeper understanding of the world.

Intimate friendships, where trust and vulnerability are at the core, provide a safe space for a leader to be themselves without the pressures of their role. Among trusted friends, a leader can share their fears, doubts, hopes, and dreams, finding solace in the shared human experience. This emotional sanctuary is essential for recharging a leader's spirit so they can face the challenges of leadership with renewed energy and resilience.

The social setting is like a big canvas where relationships are painted. It's not just about close friends, but also about acquaintances, colleagues, and mentors. A good leader needs to understand how to connect and influence people in these networks, building alliances, fostering collaboration, and inspiring others along the way. It's all about give and take - supporting and encouraging each other to keep the social ecosystem healthy.

Empathy and emotional intelligence are key in social dynamics. A leader who can understand and relate to others' feelings and motivations can navigate any challenge with grace. By being aware of what people in their network need and want, a leader can tailor their approach to offer the right kind of help and guidance. This kind of empathetic leadership builds strong bonds, trust, and respect within a community.

Friendships and social networks are like the glue that holds a leader and their community together in the tapestry of leadership. These relationships are crucial for effective leadership to take root. The more a leader invests in nurturing these connections, the stronger their network will be to support them in reaching their goals. And in the end, they'll leave behind a legacy of collaboration, empathy, and growth.

Volunteering and Community Service

Leadership is often associated with strategic planning, decision-making, and visionary foresight. However, there is another important aspect of leadership that is often overlooked: giving back through volunteering and community service. This element of leadership should not be seen as an optional extra, but rather as a fundamental principle that should guide all leaders who lead with compassion.

In every city and town, some unsung heroes dedicate their time to community service, creating a network of compassion and selflessness that binds society together. Volunteering goes beyond personal and professional life, extending its reach to influence a wider circle of people. It is through these selfless acts that leaders can truly measure their impact, not through awards or titles, but through the positive changes they inspire within their communities.

Imagine walking into a local shelter and seeing a leader trading their business suit for an apron as they serve meals to those in need. In that moment, hierarchical barriers disappear, and the essence of humanity shines through. Serving food becomes an act of solidarity and humility, where the leader gives more than just time or resources - they offer respect, dignity, and hope. This connection fosters a sense of belonging, reminding both the server and the served that they are part of a caring community.

Volunteering isn't just about helping others - it's also a great way to grow and learn more about yourself. When someone who's used to being in charge at work steps into a volunteer role, it can be a real eye-opener. It humbles them and opens their mind to different perspectives and experiences. This kind of interaction helps leaders develop empathy and understanding, which are key qualities for effective leadership.

Community service is also a fantastic way to build teamwork and strengthen bonds within a group. Whether it's planting trees, cleaning up a beach, or tutoring kids in need, working together on a common goal creates a sense of unity that goes beyond the office. These shared experiences foster a spirit of teamwork and support among colleagues, making the organization feel like a close-knit community.

Leaders who are active in community service inspire others to get involved too. Their actions set an example and encouraged others to give back to their community. This kind of ripple effect can create a culture of volunteerism within an organization or community, where giving back is a shared value. Leaders play a crucial role in creating an environment where everyone can come together to make a difference.

When leaders volunteer and serve their community, it shows their dedication to making a positive impact. It demonstrates their belief in the power of collective action and the importance of building strong social connections. Stepping out of their comfort zones and getting involved in their communities not only enriches their own lives but also leaves a lasting impression on the community.

Through their service, they embody the true essence of leading with compassion and empathy.

Mentorship and Guidance

At the heart of effective leadership lies a key principle that sets the good apart from the great - the art of mentorship and guidance. As leaders navigate the complexities of their roles, the ability to inspire, nurture, and develop others becomes crucial. It's not just about sharing knowledge; it's about fostering growth, building confidence, and leaving a legacy of empowered individuals ready to step into leadership positions.

Think of a small sapling surrounded by towering trees. Without the right conditions and attention, it won't thrive. Similarly, emerging leaders need support to grow and flourish. A good mentor recognizes this need and provides a nurturing environment for talent to blossom. Drawing from their own experiences, mentors offer wisdom and lessons learned from both successes and failures. This shared knowledge creates a foundation for mentees to learn from past paths to success and avoid potential pitfalls.

Deep listening is a key aspect of effective mentorship. By truly understanding a mentee's aspirations, fears, and challenges, mentors can help build confidence and foster meaningful dialogue. When mentees feel heard and valued, they become more open about their goals and uncertainties. This vulnerability creates space for growth and allows mentors to provide tailored guidance to support individual needs and objectives.

Guidance isn't about having all the answers, it's about asking the right questions that make you think and reflect. A good mentor knows that true learning comes from within. By challenging their mentee to come up with their solutions, they help them take ownership and responsibility. This not only improves problem-solving skills but also boosts confidence in facing future challenges independently.

The mentor-mentee relationship is always changing. It's a delicate balance between providing support and pushing for growth, giving direction while allowing space for personal exploration. A mentor must understand that everyone's journey is different, and flexibility is key to providing relevant and effective guidance.

The most rewarding part of mentoring is seeing the gradual transformation that occurs. As skills are developed, new perspectives emerge, and confidence grows, mentees begin to realize their full potential. This process is incredibly rewarding for both mentor and mentee, creating a lasting impact that extends beyond the individual and inspires others to become mentors themselves, fostering a culture of growth and support.

In a nutshell, mentorship and guidance are not just about professional development; they're about people and shared growth. They remind us that leadership is not only an individual journey but a collective one, in which we rise through the elevation of others. Mentors give leaders a big-picture view of how they have influenced not only careers but also lives, leaving a greater legacy than they could ever achieve for themselves.

Personal Growth and Fulfillment

Leaders often find themselves reflecting on their purpose and the impact they have on others during quiet moments. The leadership journey isn't just about guiding others, but also about personal growth and fulfilment. True leaders are driven by the success of their team and the growth that comes from overcoming challenges.

Self-awareness plays a crucial role in the personal growth of leaders. By understanding their strengths and areas for improvement, leaders can better connect with those they lead. This authenticity builds trust and respect, forming the foundation for meaningful relationships.

Continuous learning is essential for personal fulfilment. Leaders who remain curious and open to new experiences find themselves enriched in unexpected ways. Whether through formal education or everyday wisdom, learning is a lifelong process that enhances capabilities and sets a positive example for others.

Resilience is key to personal growth for leaders. Setbacks and failures are not roadblocks, but growth opportunities. Leaders who approach challenges with resilience can turn adversity into valuable lessons, inspiring their teams to tackle obstacles with determination.

Woven into the tapestry of fulfilment are threads of passion and purpose. Leaders who live out their core values and passions feel a deep sense of fulfilment. This alignment acts as a compass, guiding decisions and actions with clarity and integrity. When leaders lead with genuine passion and enthusiasm, they inspire their teams to do the same.

Another key aspect of authenticity is finding a balance between work and personal life. Leaders who take care of their physical, emotional, and mental well-being are better equipped to serve others. It's important to set boundaries, practice self-care, and nurture relationships outside of work. By prioritizing holistic fitness, leaders set a positive example for their teams to follow.

During busy days, leaders must take moments to reflect and express gratitude. These moments allow leaders to appreciate how far they've come, acknowledge their growth, and celebrate their accomplishments. Gratitude fosters a positive mindset and contentment, while reflection brings clarity and insight for moving forward.

Personal growth and fulfilment in leadership involve self-evolution. It's a dynamic process that includes introspection, learning, resilience, passion, balance, and gratitude.

 Leaders who fully commit to this journey not only transform their own lives but also inspire others to pursue growth and fulfilment. Leading with heart is about personal growth and guiding others toward a shared vision of success.

Chapter - 9

Ethical Implications of Servant Leadership

Moral Responsibility

Leaders are like the moral compass of their organizations, guiding everyone on what's right and wrong. They set the tone for acceptable behaviour. Being morally responsible as a leader isn't just about following a code of ethics - it's about showing principles like trust, respect, and integrity in everything you do. A leader's actions and decisions can seriously impact the lives of their employees, the culture of their organization, and even the wider community.

When a leader takes on moral responsibility, it creates a foundation for ethical behaviour to become the norm. By sticking to doing the right thing, even when it's tough, it sends a powerful message to the whole organization. Trust is key for any team to succeed, and employees are more likely to follow a leader who consistently acts ethically because it shows they care about their well-being.

A leader's morally responsible influence doesn't stop at the workplace - it can inspire others in their personal and professional lives too. This can lead to a more ethical society where people carry those principles into all aspects of life. When leaders hold themselves accountable, it helps create a culture of responsibility and integrity that spreads throughout the organization and beyond.

Being willing to make the right decisions, even when they're not the most profitable or popular, is a key part of being a leader. This means sticking to ethical standards and taking moral responsibility seriously. Sometimes, it means standing up against shady practices, fighting for fair treatment of employees, or making sure the organization is eco-friendly. It can be tough to make these choices, especially when they go against short-term goals or outside pressures.

Another big part of being a responsible leader is being transparent. This means being open about how decisions are made. Leaders should explain why they made certain choices, especially ones that have a big impact on the organization or its people. Being transparent helps employees feel included and valued, knowing their leaders are being fair and honest.

On top of making ethical decisions, leaders also need to own up to their actions and their consequences. Basically, they should admit when they mess up, learn from it, and make things right. By being accountable, leaders create a safe environment for employees to take risks, try new things, and grow. Mistakes are seen as opportunities to learn, not reasons for punishment.

Taking on moral responsibility means being dedicated to the growth and happiness of others. It's all about giving people the chance to learn and advance in their careers, creating a work environment where everyone feels safe and respected, and helping employees find a good balance between their personal and professional lives. Leaders who genuinely care about their team's well-being are more likely to inspire loyalty, motivation, and top-notch performance.

In simpler terms, being morally responsible as a leader means leading with compassion. It means sticking to ethical values, making tough decisions when necessary, being open about your actions, taking responsibility for the outcomes, and genuinely caring about the well-being of others. By embracing these principles, leaders can make a positive and lasting impact on their organizations and society as a whole.

Fairness and Justice

Fairness and justice go hand in hand when it comes to leadership. A good leader is fair, treating everyone equally and making sure opportunities are shared without any bias. They also recognize the strengths of each team member and appreciate what they bring to the table.

On the other hand, justice is all about making the right decisions based on morals. A leader needs to have integrity and be accountable for their actions, holding themselves and their team to a high standard. This creates an environment where team members feel respected and valued, encouraging them to do their best work.

When leaders involve their team in decision-making, it shows that they value their input and opinions. This collaborative effort leads to better decisions and a stronger commitment from the team. Fairness and justice aren't just about the end result, but also about the process of getting there. It's all about creating a culture of openness and transparency where everyone feels heard and respected.

A great leader knows that being fair and just is key, but empathy is just as important. They take the time to understand what challenges people are facing and try to help in the fairest and just way possible. This approach helps build strong relationships and keeps team members loyal and committed.

When conflicts arise, a fair and just leader stays calm and objective. They listen to all sides, gather all the facts, and make decisions based on what's right, not personal feelings. This helps build trust and credibility with the team as they work through disagreements.

Fairness and justice don't stop within the team - they extend to everyone the leader interacts with, like clients, partners, and the community. By treating everyone fairly, the leader helps build a good reputation for the organization and maintains strong relationships.

To truly be fair and just, a leader needs to reflect on their own biases and be open to feedback and change. It's all about creating a positive, inclusive environment where everyone can succeed. Leading with compassion and respect makes a real difference and leaves a legacy of integrity and respect.

Transparency and Accountability

In the ever-changing world of leadership, transparency and accountability are the key ingredients for building trust within teams. Transparency is all about being open and honest, making sure that leaders' intentions, decisions, and actions are clear to everyone. This helps team members feel informed and involved in the journey, creating a culture of open communication.

Accountability goes hand in hand with transparency, ensuring that actions align with words. It's about taking responsibility for both successes and failures and setting a good example for the team. Owning up to mistakes is important, as it allows for growth and continuous improvement.

Transparency without accountability can lead to mistrust, while accountability without transparency can create fear and suspicion. Together, they create a balanced and healthy organizational culture where communication flows freely and mistakes are seen as opportunities for learning.

Implementing effective communication strategies within a team can be achieved in various ways. Communication must be consistent and transparent. Leaders can organize town hall meetings, send out newsletters, or use digital media platforms to share updates and gather feedback. These communication channels should encourage two-way conversations and recognize the contributions of team members.

Transparency is key when it comes to decision-making processes within leadership. Leaders need to explain why certain strategic decisions were made and what criteria will determine their success or failure. Sharing performance metrics and organizational goals with team members helps them understand what is expected of them and how their efforts contribute to the overall objectives of the organization.

Regular reviews and feedback sessions are essential for fostering a culture of continuous improvement. Feedback should be constructive and focused on moving forward, rather than dwelling on past mistakes. Leaders should also demonstrate accountability by openly acknowledging their mistakes and outlining steps they are taking to rectify them. This not only shows integrity but also encourages a culture of learning and growth within the team.

Fostering transparency and accountability within a company's culture involves encouraging and rewarding behaviours that promote openness and responsibility. Recognizing and celebrating team members who exemplify these qualities helps reinforce the importance of these values to everyone else.

Transparency and accountability are not just nice ideas, they are practical tools that can transform leadership. By creating an environment of trust and empowerment, team members become more engaged and the organization becomes more resilient in the face of challenges. These principles allow leaders to lead authentically and build a culture based on honesty, responsibility, and respect for one another.

Respecting Diversity

Recognizing and valuing diversity is crucial in today's ever-changing leadership landscape. Successful leaders don't just accept differences, they actively seek to understand and celebrate them. By creating an inclusive workplace, they foster a culture where everyone feels valued, respected, and empowered to share their unique perspectives and talents.

An essential aspect of an inclusive culture is the leader's ability to listen actively and empathetically. This means truly hearing and considering each team member's input without bias or judgment, creating a safe space for open communication. Leaders who excel in this skill benefit from a wealth of diverse ideas and viewpoints, leading to innovative solutions and outcomes.

By embracing and appreciating the diverse cultural backgrounds and experiences of team members, leaders can foster deeper connections and understanding. This goes beyond surface-level interactions, demonstrating a genuine interest in learning about different traditions, values, and customs. This not only broadens a leader's perspective but also shows a profound respect for the diversity within the team.

In addition, it is essential for leaders to actively combat discrimination and prejudice within the workplace. This requires vigilant leadership, proactively addressing any behaviours or practices that hinder inclusivity. Implementing anti-discrimination policies, providing diversity training, and encouraging open discussions on these topics are effective ways to promote a culture of respect and equality.

Ultimately, the message conveyed by leadership is clear - every team member is valued and respected. By prioritizing inclusivity and diversity, leaders can create a positive and supportive work environment where everyone can thrive.

It's super important for a leader to recognize their own biases and work hard to overcome them. They need to be self-aware and reflect on their actions regularly, as well as ask for feedback from others. By acknowledging and trying to get rid of their biases, leaders can show their team how to do the same.

Leaders should also make sure their team is inclusive and diverse. They need to push for a mix of people in the organization, from different backgrounds and experiences. This means making sure there are minorities in leadership roles and giving more people a say in decision-making. By championing these initiatives, leaders can create a fair and inclusive workplace that benefits everyone.

Diversity isn't just about race or gender - it includes a whole range of differences like age, preferences, abilities, and backgrounds. Leaders need to have a broad definition of diversity to make sure everyone feels seen and valued.

Respecting diversity isn't a one-time thing - it's an ongoing commitment. Leaders need to keep an open mind, keep learning, and be open to different perspectives. By making this commitment, leaders can create a welcoming and inclusive environment where everyone has a chance to succeed.

In the end, leading with heart means embracing all the different aspects of human nature and appreciating the unique contributions each person can bring. Leaders who do this will foster a culture of mutual respect, leading to increased collaboration, innovation, and success.

Long-term Impact

True leadership has a ripple effect that goes beyond just the present moment, shaping the future in a lasting way. When leaders embody empathy, integrity, and authenticity, their influence becomes a legacy that lasts long after they're gone. This isn't by chance, but rather a reflection of the values a leader brings and instills in others.

Think about how leadership impacts the culture of an organization. Leaders who lead with their hearts create environments where trust, respect, and open communication thrive. These principles lay the groundwork for innovation and collaboration to flourish. When employees feel valued, understood, and motivated, they become more satisfied with their jobs and more productive. Over time, these values become ingrained in the organization's DNA, shaping how business is conducted and challenges are approached.

Another crucial aspect of this enduring leadership is the development of future leaders. Leaders who mentor with empathy and provide growth opportunities inspire others to follow in their footsteps. They cultivate a pipeline of individuals with technical skills, motivation, and a sense of direction guided by ethical responsibility. This continuity ensures that the organization's values and visions are preserved and advanced for future generations, creating a culture of leadership that is sustainable and resilient.

The impact of having socially responsible leaders goes beyond just the organizations themselves. When leaders act ethically, it benefits the communities they are a part of. These leaders support causes they care about and inspire others to make positive contributions to society. They can do this through corporate social responsibility, community involvement, or other ways of promoting causes. As the ripple effect spreads throughout the communities, it improves the lives of others, creating a cycle of goodness.

Personal growth within individuals in the organization is also a testament to the long-term impact of leading with compassion. People who work in an environment that fosters growth and care often develop high self-esteem and confidence. This personal growth empowers them to take on new challenges, pursue their goals, and make a difference in their communities. As these employees progress in life, they carry the lessons and values instilled in them by their leaders, continuing the cycle of positivity.

Heart-led leadership also leaves a lasting impression on the organization's reputation. Ethical practices, compassionate leadership, and a commitment to social responsibility attract like-minded individuals and partners. This builds trust and loyalty among customers and clients, ensuring a long-lasting relationship with the organization. The goodwill generated by such leadership extends far into the future and sets the organization apart from its competitors.

In the grand scheme of things, passionate leaders play a crucial role in shaping the future. They serve as role models, guiding individuals and organizations towards success with integrity, compassion, and excellence. The impact of leading with heart is significant and enduring, showcasing the importance of empathy and authenticity in making a positive difference in the world.

Chapter - 10
Promoting Collaboration and Teamwork

Creating a Collaborative Environment

The room is buzzing with energy, filled with a symphony of voices and occasional bursts of laughter. Sunlight pours in through large windows, casting a warm glow on a massive oval table surrounded by an eclectic mix of chairs. Colourful artwork and whiteboards covered in notes of every colour adorn the walls, showcasing the creativity and passion that emanate from this space. It's a hub for collaboration, meticulously designed to foster open communication and mutual respect.

As you step into the room, you immediately feel a sense of belonging. Trust and shared purpose hang in the air, with each voice valued equally and every idea met with respect. The leader, exuding quiet confidence, sits among peers rather than above them, creating an inviting atmosphere that encourages free expression and the sharing of unique ideas.

The leader kicks off discussions not with answers, but with questions. "What projects are you working on? What challenges are you facing? What successes have you had?" And then, they listen. Participants engage in active listening, making eye contact, nodding in agreement, and offering thoughtful responses or follow-up questions. Everyone knows their words will be heard and considered.

In this environment, there's no fear of expressing opinions. Ideas are met with respect and curiosity, rather than criticism. Through exploration and collaboration, ideas are dissected and built upon, creating a culture of learning and innovation. Mistakes are seen as opportunities for growth, fostering a mindset of continuous improvement.

Overall, this space is a vibrant and dynamic place where creativity thrives, ideas are valued, and collaboration is key. It's a place where everyone's voice is heard, and where learning and innovation are at the forefront.

The collaborative vibe in our workspace is top-notch. We've got cosy seating that encourages face-to-face interaction, no barriers like desks or podiums to keep us apart, and whiteboards and flip charts galore for some serious brainstorming. Plus, we're fully equipped with all the latest tech to make sure our remote team members feel just as connected as those in the room.

Diversity and inclusivity are key around here. Our leader knows that different perspectives lead to better ideas and stronger solutions. They make sure everyone has a chance to speak up, even the quieter folks, so no one gets overshadowed.

Trust is the name of the game in our office. It's built on consistent actions and reinforced daily. Our leader walks the talk with integrity, transparency, and genuine care for each team member. This trust creates a safe space where we can take risks and know we've got support from our leader and colleagues.

As the meeting progresses, a feeling of getting closer to a resolution grows. Ideas are coming together to form actionable plans, and responsibilities are being assigned based on strengths and interests. A shared vision is starting to take shape. The leader ensures that every team member leaves the room feeling valued, acknowledged, and motivated to work towards the same goal. This is more than just a meeting; it's a glimpse into a collaborative environment where passion and logic come together to achieve shared objectives.

Team Building Activities

In leadership, activities are the glue that brings a tight team together, going beyond just exercises to build trust, understanding, and unity. Leading with Heart emphasizes the importance of team building as a key element in creating an environment where people not only work together but thrive together.

Picture a group of employees out in nature, away from the noise and chaos of the office. There's a sense of excitement and curiosity in the air. This setting is intentional, setting the stage for the activities about to take place.

First up, the Trust Fall: each team member takes a turn falling backwards into their colleagues' arms. There's hesitation, anxiety, and then finally, a moment of surrender as they trust their team to catch them. It's a simple yet powerful exercise that lays the foundation for trust within the team.

Next, a problem-solving challenge inspired by an Escape Room. Teammates are locked in a room and must work together to find clues and solve puzzles to escape. This activity not only promotes teamwork but also showcases individual strengths and how they complement each other. From the analytical thinker to the creative mind to the low-key leader, each person plays a vital role in the team's success.

The shared adrenaline rush of solving the final puzzle, the collective sigh of relief, and the high of success all come together to bond the team uniquely. These activities not only build trust and unity but also highlight the diverse strengths and talents within the team.

Imagine stepping into a quiet conference room and being greeted by The Story Circle activity. Here, team members are invited to share personal stories that have shaped who they are today - from moments of triumph to instances of vulnerability. As each story is shared, empathy and understanding grow among the group. The reserved coworker opens up about overcoming difficulties, while the cheerful teammate reveals a moment of loss. These revelations break down barriers and create genuine connections.

Physical activities are also key, like team-based scavenger hunts in parks or urban areas. Teams must navigate, strategize, and work together to find hidden items or complete tasks. The laughter, friendly competition, and spontaneous creativity help strengthen bonds. Running through the park, solving clues, and celebrating victories create lasting memories and reinforce friendships.

Each activity, whether focused on trust, problem-solving, storytelling, or physical collaboration, serves a purpose. They aren't just for entertainment, but to deepen connections among teammates. These shared experiences and mutual respect form the foundation of a cohesive team. According to Leading with Heart, these activities are essential for leaders looking to build a successful team that works well together and achieves greatness.

Shared Goals and Vision

In the soft morning light, a group of people gathers in a bright, spacious room. Their eyes shine with a shared purpose, their hearts beating as one. They are brought together by a vision that transcends their diverse backgrounds and experiences.

The leader in front isn't a bossy figure, but a mentor who understands that true leadership is about unity and teamwork. They know that strength comes from working together towards a common goal, rather than trying to suppress individual differences.

The room buzzes with energy, as everyone's personal goals align with the organization's objectives. It's in this harmony that the magic happens. Each person brings their unique skills and perspectives to the table, enriching the collective vision.

The air is filled with the aroma of coffee, and quiet conversations fill the room as plans are shared. Ideas are written on the walls, evolving and taking new shapes. The leader listens attentively, taking in everything happening around them.

They understand that a collective vision is not isolated, but a beautiful mosaic woven from individual dreams and aspirations. It's about coming together, appreciating each other's contributions, and working towards a common goal.

The leader's words act as a soothing balm, lifting the spirits of the people and instilling confidence and determination in them. They speak of a future that is within reach, where their efforts will pay off. The voice is filled with experience and wisdom, having navigated the challenges of leadership successfully. But it is also filled with optimism, believing in the potential of the human spirit.

In this space, the leader plants the seeds of a vision with care. These seeds can only grow with trust, open communication, and mutual respect. The leader encourages them to dream big, set high goals, and believe in the impossible. A shared vision goes beyond just setting goals; it gives a sense of direction and a reason to strive for something greater.

As the meeting ends, you can feel the anticipation in the air. The leader looks into the eyes of each member, silently expressing gratitude and solidarity. It's not just about meeting objectives, but about growing together, learning from each other, and creating something greater as a team.

The shared vision takes flight on the wings of hope and determination. It guides them through the challenges and successes that lie ahead. As they leave the room, their hearts are full of purpose and their minds are clear. They are united by a common dream that will lead them to endless possibilities.

Celebrating Team Successes

The office was buzzing with energy, a clear sign of the hard work and dedication each team member put in. Meeting milestones wasn't just about hitting targets, but also about recognizing the teamwork that got them there. The conference room was decked out with colourful banners celebrating the names and achievements of top performers, filling the air with pride, relief, and joy.

The committee sat around a large table, beaming with pride at their success. The leader, grinning from ear to ear, was ready to address the team. From snacks to personalized thank-you notes, every detail of the celebration showed just how much their success meant. This wasn't just a meeting, but a celebration of the passion and effort poured into their work.

The leader began by recounting the journey that led them to this moment. They shared stories of challenges faced, obstacles overcome, and doubts turned into victories. Each team member was recognized and appreciated through heartfelt speeches. Applause filled the room with each achievement mentioned, highlighting the strong bond formed over time.

As the leader continued, they emphasized the importance of acknowledging both big and small wins. Success wasn't always flashy or grand, sometimes it was found in the quiet dedication of working late into the night or in finding innovative solutions to project roadblocks. These seemingly small moments were the foundation of their collective success. The leader's words inspired unity and a shared sense of purpose among the team.

It was a time for looking back and looking ahead. He encouraged everyone to keep pushing themselves, breaking boundaries, and exploring new opportunities. The potential ahead was fuelled by the same passion and commitment that had brought them this far. The future was bright, waiting to be shaped.

As the event wrapped up, team members shared stories and laughs, strengthening their bonds even further. They celebrated their successes, knowing that it was the combined effort of every team member that had led to their achievements.

The leader took a moment to reflect on the importance of these celebrations. They were more than just a pat on the back - they were essential for building a close-knit, strong team. Each success served as a reminder of what they could accomplish together, reinforcing the values they lived by.

Celebrating team successes became a powerful tool for creating a positive work environment. It was a chance to show appreciation for the hard work and dedication of each member, recognizing the obstacles they had overcome and inspiring them to keep going. With each celebration, the team's spirit grew stronger - proof that leading with heart truly makes a difference.

Handling Team Conflicts

Managing team dynamics can be a real challenge, especially when personalities clash and opinions differ. But believe it or not, these conflicts can actually be a good thing. They can help team members understand each other better and ultimately make the group stronger. This is where effective leadership comes into play - recognizing that conflict can lead to positive change.

The first step in resolving conflicts is promoting open communication within the team. Leaders need to create a safe space for team members to share their thoughts and concerns without fear of backlash. It's all about active listening and making sure everyone feels heard and understood.

Identifying the root cause of the conflict is crucial. Every disagreement has a deeper reason behind it, whether it's a misunderstanding or unmet expectations. Leaders need to be patient and non-judgmental as they work to uncover these underlying issues through discussions or feedback mechanisms.

Mediation is also key in resolving conflicts. Having a neutral party facilitate a conversation between the conflicting parties can help them find common ground and reach a compromise. This can foster empathy among team members and lead to long-term resolutions.

By approaching conflicts with empathy and a willingness to understand each other's perspectives, teams can overcome disagreements and become stronger as a result.

Dealing with conflicts in a team isn't a one-size-fits-all kind of thing. Every situation is different, and so are the people involved. Sometimes you might need to bring in HR or outside mediators, while other times a team-building activity or problem-solving session can do the trick.

The key to building a strong team is learning from conflicts. After a conflict, take some time to think about what caused it, how it was handled, and what could have been done differently. This reflection not only helps prevent similar issues in the future but also improves the team's ability to handle conflicts effectively.

Leaders play a big role in setting the tone for how conflicts are handled. By staying calm, being fair, and focusing on finding solutions, leaders can show their team how to deal with conflicts gracefully. When team members see their leader handling conflicts well, they're more likely to follow suit.

It's also important to recognize and celebrate when conflicts are resolved in a positive way. By highlighting the benefits of reaching a resolution, teams are motivated to handle future conflicts constructively.

Overall, dealing with conflicts in a compassionate and strategic way not only solves immediate problems but also strengthens the team. By turning conflicts into learning opportunities, teams can grow and collaborate more effectively.

Chapter - 11

Developing Effective Communication Skills

Active Listening Techniques

In the world of leadership, one of the most important skills is truly listening to others. Being an effective leader means actively listening, which goes beyond just hearing words - it's about connecting with the person speaking on a deeper level. Active listening requires making a conscious effort to focus entirely on the speaker, understand their message, respond thoughtfully, and remember what was said. This skill can greatly help a leader connect with their team, build trust, and drive success.

To practice active listening, start by physically listening - turn off distractions, make eye contact, and use body language to show you're paying attention. Stay in the moment and avoid thinking about your response while the other person is talking. Your body language, like leaning forward and keeping an open posture, shows that you value and respect what the other person is saying.

The next layer of active listening is cognitive, which involves processing and understanding the speaker's perspective. This can be done by paraphrasing or summarizing what was said to confirm understanding. For example, you could say, "It sounds like you're feeling overwhelmed by the project deadlines. Is that right?" These responses not only show that you've understood the message but also validate the speaker's feelings and concerns.

Active listening involves more than just hearing words - it requires empathy. It means being able to understand how someone feels about what they're saying and responding in a way that shows you care about their emotions. A good listener, especially a leader, can connect emotionally with someone by acknowledging their feelings of frustration or excitement. This helps the person feel valued and understood, which can lead to more open and honest communication.

Asking open-ended questions is another key aspect of active listening. Instead of asking simple yes or no questions, a leader should ask questions that encourage the speaker to share more details and thoughts. For example, instead of asking "Are you happy with the project?" a leader could ask "What do you think about this project so far?" This not only helps gather more information but also shows genuine interest in the speaker's opinions and experiences.

Reflective listening is another effective skill in active listening. This involves repeating what the speaker has said in a similar tone and emotional manner. It can be especially helpful in emotional situations, as it shows the speaker that you understand both their words and their feelings. For example, a leader might say "It sounds like you are very passionate about this new initiative," reflecting both the content and the speaker's enthusiasm.

By practising active listening techniques like empathy, open-ended questions, and reflective listening, leaders can create a more supportive and understanding environment for their team members. This can lead to better communication, stronger relationships, and ultimately, more successful outcomes.

Active listening is not just sitting back and nodding your head; it's about being engaged and responsive. It requires practice, patience, and a genuine curiosity about others. When leaders excel at active listening, they can foster a more inclusive, cooperative, and encouraging environment. This enables leaders to better comprehend their team's needs, approach challenges with a more attentive mindset, and guide their teams with empathy and understanding. Whether it's in one-on-one interactions or within an entire organization, active listening ensures that everyone's voice is heard and their perspectives are respected.

Non-Verbal Communication

Nonverbal communication, also known as body language, is a crucial aspect of effective leadership. This silent form of communication can either enhance or hinder interactions and perceptions. Leaders who can interpret and utilize nonverbal cues effectively can convey confidence, empathy, and trustworthiness without uttering a single word.

One of the most powerful forms of nonverbal communication is eye contact. Maintaining eye contact during conversations demonstrates attentiveness, honesty, and respect for the other person. For leaders, making proper eye contact with team members reassures them that their thoughts and contributions are valued. Conversely, avoiding eye contact can be interpreted as disinterest or evasiveness, potentially damaging a leader's credibility.

Facial expressions also play a significant role in nonverbal communication. A genuine smile can create a welcoming atmosphere and foster camaraderie. On the other hand, furrowed brows or a frown can signal unhappiness or confusion, hindering effective communication. Leaders must be mindful of their facial expressions, as they often speak louder than words.

Gestures are another important aspect of nonverbal communication. Open gestures, such as spreading arms or showing palms, convey openness and honesty. Conversely, crossed arms may be perceived as defensive or closed off. Leaders can use gestures to emphasize their verbal messages and keep communication engaging and dynamic.

In conclusion, mastering nonverbal communication is essential for effective leadership. By understanding and utilizing body language cues, leaders can enhance their communication skills and build stronger relationships with their team members.

Posture says a lot about a person's confidence and authority. Standing tall and straight shows strength and assurance, while slouching or leaning back can make you seem uninterested or unsure. If you're a leader, it's important to always keep a good posture, especially in important situations, to show that you're capable and in control.

Another important non-verbal cue is proxemics, which is all about personal space. The distance you keep from others during interactions can make them feel more or less comfortable and engaged. Standing too close can be invasive while standing too far away might make you seem uncaring. It's all about finding the right balance for effective and comfortable communication.

Using touch in the right way can also be powerful. A firm handshake can show warmth and respect, while a pat on the back can be encouraging and supportive. Just make sure to be aware of cultural differences and personal boundaries to avoid making anyone feel uncomfortable or misunderstood.

The tone of voice is a powerful non-verbal characteristic that can have a big impact on communication. Sometimes how something is said is more important than what is said. A calm and soothing tone can make people feel at ease, while a harsh or rushed tone can cause confusion or upset. Leaders need to be mindful of how they speak to effectively get their message across.

Non-verbal communication is a complex and ever-changing aspect of leadership. It requires a deep understanding of oneself and others. By using non-verbal cues effectively, leaders can create a positive and productive work environment, improve relationships, and connect with their team members on a deeper level. Mastering non-verbal communication is not just a bonus for leaders, it's a must-have skill for those who want to lead with compassion and empathy.

Constructive Feedback

Providing feedback is like a fine art in the world of leadership. It's a crucial part of personal and organizational growth. It's not just something managers have to do - it's a fantastic chance to help people improve, learn new skills, and create a culture of always getting better. When feedback is given in a positive and caring way, it can make a difference and motivate people to reach their full potential.

Imagine a boss who notices that one of their team members is having a tough time with a certain task. Instead of getting mad or giving orders, this boss decides to handle things differently. They ask for a private meeting to make sure the team member feels comfortable and at ease. The first thing they do is genuinely thank the team members for all the hard work they've put in so far. This sets a positive tone right from the start. It's not just empty praise - it's a real recognition of the value that person brings to the team.

Next, the boss gets into the heart of the feedback by talking about the specific issue they've noticed, instead of making general comments. For example, instead of saying "Your reports are bad," they might say "I've noticed some inconsistencies in the way data is presented in your recent reports." Being specific helps the team members understand exactly what needs to improve and keeps them focused on the goal, which reduces the chances of misunderstandings or conflicts.

Feedback should always focus on behaviour, not on the person. It's important to separate someone's actions from who they are as a person. The goal is to help them improve, not criticize their character. For example, a leader could say, "I think if you pay a little more attention to detail, your reports will meet our high standards without getting personal."

Good feedback should include an action plan. A leader might suggest additional training, provide helpful tools, or offer to review the next report together. This shows that the leader is invested in the team member's development and provides a clear path forward.

It's also important for the leader to invite discussion. By encouraging the team member to share their perspective, a dialogue is created. This not only helps identify issues but also encourages the team member to take ownership of their development. The leader should listen actively, show empathy, and respect the team member's opinions.

Throughout the feedback process, the leader should be supportive and positive. By believing in the team member's potential for improvement and success, the leader can motivate them and strengthen their partnership in their growth journey.

Receiving feedback can make a difference. When a leader and team members trust and respect each other, it creates a positive environment where feedback is seen as a way to improve, not as a form of punishment. This leads to team members being more open to feedback, actively seeking it out, and being dedicated to their growth.

In the world of leadership, constructive feedback is like a supportive thread woven with empathy and clarity. It helps turn challenges into opportunities and strengthens the bonds within a team. Leaders not only improve individual performance but also cultivate an organization that is thriving, dynamic, and resilient thanks to this important concept.

Clarity and Conciseness

The art of leading with heart is powerful in its simplicity and elegance. Imagine a calm lake, so clear that you can see every pebble and ripple beneath the surface. That's the kind of transparency effective leaders aim for in their communication.

A leader's words are like brushstrokes on the canvas of their team's collective mind. Each word is carefully chosen, and each message is crafted to create understanding and harmony. When clarity reigns, confusion disappears like morning mist in the sun.

Conciseness is the opposite - distilling complexity into essence. It's about saying a lot with a few words, leaving a lasting impression. Picture a block of marble and a skilled sculptor: with each chisel stroke, they reveal the beautiful form by removing the unnecessary.

Clear and concise leaders respect their team's time and intelligence. They understand that deciphering a confusing message takes away from productivity and engagement. By providing clarity, they empower their team to take action instead of wasting time trying to interpret vague instructions.

Imagine a team meeting where a new project is on the table. The leader speaks with such clarity that everyone knows exactly what needs to be done and why. There's no confusion and no room for misinterpretation. The team is engaged, not because they have to ask a million questions, but because the leader gets straight to the point.

The leader doesn't waste time with long speeches or repeating themselves. Every word is carefully chosen, and every point is made with precision. The meeting ends on a high note, with everyone ready to tackle the next steps.

This magic of clear communication doesn't stop at spoken words. It flows into written messages, presentations, and even active listening. Leaders ensure their team feels heard and understood, respecting their time and attention.

In a world full of information overload, leaders who can communicate clearly and concisely shine like beacons of light. Their messages cut through the noise; their intentions crystal clear. They build trust and understanding, creating a culture where every voice matters.

In the journey of leadership, clarity and conciseness aren't just tools - they're essential. They turn leaders into visionaries, guiding their teams with a steady hand and an open heart. By communicating effectively, leaders inspire confidence, foster cooperation, and pave the way for success.

Public Speaking Skills

Public speaking is an art that can inspire, persuade, and connect people on a deeper level. It is a crucial skill for any leader looking to effectively communicate their vision, values, and strategies. Speaking to a crowd involves more than just words; it's about using voice modulation, body language, and emotional intelligence to create a powerful impact.

Picture yourself standing in front of a sea of faces, all eyes on you, eager to hear what you have to say. Your heart is racing, your palms might be sweaty, and your mind is racing. But this moment is full of potential. The first step to becoming a great public speaker is understanding your audience: who they are, what they believe in, and what they need from your message. This empathy is key to effective communication and helps you craft a speech that resonates deeply with your listeners.

Preparation is essential for a successful speech. Start by jotting down the key points you want to make. A strong opening can captivate your audience right from the start. This could be a story, a question, or some surprising statistics to grab their attention. The body of your speech should flow logically, with each point leading smoothly to the next, culminating in a powerful conclusion.

Practice is just as important as preparation. Rehearse in front of a mirror or record yourself to uncover any delivery nuances. Pay attention to your tone of voice, varying it to keep your audience engaged and emphasize important points. Don't forget the power of a well-timed pause; it gives your audience time to digest information and underscores the importance of what you're saying.

Non-verbal communication is a key player in the world of public speaking. Gestures, eye contact, and facial expressions can either boost or hinder the message you're trying to convey. Having open and confident body language helps you connect with your audience and shows that you're serious about what you're saying. Making eye contact with different parts of the crowd can make them feel more engaged and included.

Dealing with nerves is another important aspect of public speaking. Even the pros get jittery sometimes; combat this by taking deep breaths, visualizing success, and giving yourself a pep talk. Think of your speech as a chat rather than a performance to ease some of the pressure. It's all about sharing ideas and connecting with your audience, not about delivering a flawless monologue.

Feedback is a valuable tool in the public speaking game. Constructive criticism from trusted colleagues and mentors can point out areas for improvement and highlight what you're doing right. Being open to feedback and willing to make changes is a sign of a dedicated speaker.

Authenticity is the cornerstone of effective public speaking. Audiences can tell if you're being genuine or putting on a show. Speaking from the heart, sharing personal stories, and staying true to your values helps build trust and credibility. Authenticity creates a bond between you and your audience, setting the stage for a lasting impact.

At its core, public speaking is more about making connections, inspiring change, and leading with conviction than just sharing information. It's a dynamic mix of words, emotions, and presence that, when mastered, can elevate a leader's ability to influence and motivate others.

Chapter - 12

Fostering Innovation and Creativity

Encouraging Creative Thinking

We live in a world where being innovative and creative is super important. As a leader, it's not just about getting your team to reach their goals, but also about creating an environment where new ideas can thrive. This means making sure your team feels comfortable sharing their thoughts without worrying about being judged. When leaders do this, they can bring out the best in their team, boosting productivity and keeping everyone motivated.

To encourage creative thinking, start by actually listening to your team. Good listening isn't just about hearing words, it's about understanding the emotions and intentions behind them. When your team feels heard and valued, they're more likely to come up with awesome ideas. Ask open-ended questions, give feedback, and show appreciation for all the input you receive.

Creating the right physical and psychological environment is also key. A well-lit workspace with stimulating elements can boost creativity. Natural light, comfy seating, and tools like whiteboards can make a big difference. But most importantly, make sure your team feels safe to take risks and make mistakes without fear of consequences. This kind of setting can encourage experimentation and the free flow of ideas.

Collaboration is super important for coming up with cool new ideas. When you bring together people from different backgrounds and perspectives, magic can happen. Leaders should make sure their teams have lots of chances to work together, like brainstorming sessions, projects that involve different departments, and spontaneous meetings where ideas can flow freely. Working together helps break down barriers and opens up new possibilities.

Giving team members ownership and freedom to take charge of their work is key to sparking innovation. When people are trusted to explore their ideas and make decisions, they can let their creativity shine. It's way better than being micromanaged and feeling stifled. Leaders should set clear goals, but also give their teams some flexibility in how they reach them.

Recognizing and rewarding creative efforts is a great way to keep the creative juices flowing. When team members see that their ideas are valued, they're more likely to keep thinking outside the box and sharing their thoughts. Whether it's through a formal recognition program, public shoutouts, or small tokens of appreciation, showing gratitude for creativity can go a long way in keeping the innovation train chugging along.

They will also be investing in further learning and development with their teams. Workshops, training programs, and other resources that foster creative skills are truly invaluable. By encouraging team members to pursue their interests and expand their knowledge in areas they are passionate about, new insights and ideas often emerge that benefit the organization as a whole.

In simpler terms, developing creative thinking is all about actively listening, creating a supportive environment, promoting teamwork, allowing for freedom, recognizing hard work, and investing in growth. When leaders prioritize these factors, it creates an atmosphere where creative thinking can flourish, leading to innovation and ultimately, success.

Creating a Safe Space for Ideas

The room was cosy and warm as the team gathered around the large wooden table, sipping on freshly brewed coffee and feeling the excitement in the air. The leader was calm and welcoming, setting the stage for a session that was sure to be life-changing. Instead of judgment, there was encouragement in the room, with everyone eager to dive into the world of innovation.

It all starts with trust, creating an environment where every voice is heard and valued. The leader understood the importance of balancing the strengths and perspectives of each team member. He made it clear that everyone's contribution was essential to the group's success. Diversity of thought and experience was celebrated, setting the stage for a culture where ideas could flow freely.

The room was set up for comfort and collaboration, with cosy seating and a round table symbolizing equality. The soft lighting created a peaceful atmosphere, while inspirational quotes and artwork on the walls served as gentle reminders of the power of creativity and thinking outside the box.

As the meeting kicked off, the leader was all ears: she made eye contact, nodded in agreement, and repeated back what she heard to make sure she got it right. This not only showed that she valued what everyone had to say, but also proved that she was really listening and considering all the ideas being shared. The leader's focus made the team feel like their thoughts were not only welcome, but crucial to the group's success.

She encouraged a culture of asking questions, letting everyone know that it was okay not to have all the answers. Instead of expecting a response, questions were seen as a way to spark curiosity and explore new possibilities. What if we looked at this problem from a different angle? How can we make this idea even better? Questions like these pushed team members to think deeper and push past the usual ways of doing things.

Creating a safe environment was key. The leader made it clear that making mistakes was not only okay, but actually encouraged as part of the creative process. By sharing personal stories of failures and lessons learned, he showed that taking risks was a natural part of growth. This helped team members feel more comfortable taking bold steps without fear of judgment.

Inclusivity was also a top priority. The leader made sure to give a voice to those who were more reserved, often directly asking for input from those who seemed hesitant to speak up. This balanced out the conversation and prevented stronger personalities from dominating. The leader ran the meeting so smoothly that everyone felt their ideas were valued and respected as soon as they were shared.

The room was alive with energy and enthusiasm as ideas flowed freely. The leader's dedication to creating a safe space for brainstorming had transformed the team into a united and innovative powerhouse. In this supportive environment, creativity flourished, paving the way for groundbreaking solutions to take root and grow into the fruits of our collective success.

Supporting Risk-Taking

Leadership is like a complex dance, where creating an environment for people to take risks is both risky and crucial. It's all about finding the right balance between pushing people to think outside the box and supporting them when things don't go as planned. Leading from the heart means fostering a culture that not only accepts but embraces calculated risks.

Imagine a workplace where ideas flow freely and creativity is not just encouraged, but actively pursued. Only leaders who understand the importance of supporting risk-taking can create such an environment. They know that true innovation requires stepping out of your comfort zone and exploring uncharted territory. Mistakes are seen as opportunities to learn and grow together as a team.

As a leader, your role is multifaceted. Building trust is key. Without trust, fear can paralyze creativity and prevent people from taking those bold, innovative steps. It's crucial to create an environment where leaders are open and vulnerable, showing that it's okay to think outside the box and challenge the status quo. Sharing personal stories of failure and resilience humanizes leadership and reinforces the idea that imperfection is just part of the journey to excellence.

Furthermore, exceptional leaders set the stage for their team members to step out of their comfort zones by providing the necessary resources and support systems. This can come in the form of training, mentorship, or access to the right tools and technologies. By arming their teams with these resources, leaders in still confidence and empower them to take calculated risks. This confidence is further bolstered when a culture of continuous learning and development is fostered, making team members feel more equipped to tackle challenges.

Recognition and rewards also play a crucial role in encouraging risk-taking. By celebrating both successes and the lessons learned from failures, leaders emphasize the value of effort and creativity above all else. Whether through formal recognition or simply acknowledging innovative courage, leaders can cultivate an environment where team members are inspired to think outside the box.

Effective communication is another key component in promoting a culture of risk-taking. Open, transparent communication removes the fear associated with taking risks. Leaders who communicate a clear, consistent vision provide direction and motivation for their teams. By creating spaces for discussion and collaboration, leaders can tap into the collective intelligence of the group to navigate potential risks.

Integrating a risk-taking mindset into the fabric of leadership influences team dynamics and organizational culture. It requires a deep understanding of human behaviour, the creation of a supportive environment built on trust, and a commitment to growth and innovation. By leading with empathy and compassion, leaders can cultivate an ecosystem where risk-taking is not only accepted but encouraged, leading to groundbreaking achievements and transformative success.

Recognizing Creative Contributions

In the hustle and bustle of the modern workplace, creativity can often be overlooked. But for leaders who lead with their hearts, recognizing and nurturing creative contributions is essential. They understand that there is more to their team members than meets the eye and that tapping into their innovative ideas can bring great value to the table.

Acknowledging creative contributions means being able to appreciate the diverse perspectives and ideas that each team member brings. It requires creating an environment where creativity is not just accepted, but encouraged. A space where team members feel comfortable sharing their thoughts, no matter how unconventional they may seem. This kind of atmosphere fosters openness and trust, allowing creativity to flourish without the fear of criticism.

Leaders with heart have a keen eye for spotting creativity in its many forms. They understand that creative contributions can come in small, subtle ways that may not always be obvious. Whether it's a new approach to an old task, a fresh idea in a brainstorming session, or a unique solution to a problem, they recognize the value that each creative endeavour brings to the table.

By paying attention to the details and encouraging creativity in all its forms, these leaders can harness the full potential of their team members. They know that every creative spark, no matter how small, can make a significant impact on the success of their endeavours.

Recognizing creativity is super important when it comes to being a great leader. Leaders who care make sure to give props and celebrate the creative efforts of their team members. This could be as simple as a nice note of appreciation, a shoutout during team meetings, or giving team members a chance to show off their ideas and projects. It not only shows that you appreciate their hard work but also inspire others to get in touch with their creative side.

On top of that, valuing creativity means providing helpful feedback. Leaders who lead with heart see creativity as a journey towards perfection. They offer advice and suggestions to help refine and improve the creative ideas of their team members. This feedback is given with empathy and respect, to nurture their creative spirit rather than squash it. By doing this, they help individuals grow and become more innovative and always learning.

Empowerment is another key aspect. Leaders who believe in creativity empower their team members by letting them explore and try new things. They give them the resources and support they need, encouraging them to take risks and step into uncharted territory. This kind of empowerment creates a sense of ownership and pride, motivating team members to give their all creatively.

Recognizing creativity doesn't just benefit individuals - it also creates a dynamic and energetic team environment where creativity is seen as a group advantage. Team members feel respected and valued, which boosts their engagement and productivity. Ideas are more likely to be shared, leading to creative solutions being found more easily.

Putting heart first means understanding that creativity is essential for driving innovation and progress. Recognizing the creative talents of individuals within a team is crucial for achieving success as a whole. When we acknowledge and appreciate creativity, we unlock new possibilities for a brighter and more innovative future.

Implementing Innovative Solutions

In any organization, adoption, growth, and innovation are key. Using innovative solutions shouldn't just be about beating the competition, but also about creating an environment that welcomes and promotes creativity and vision. Leading organizations understand that innovation is a team effort, requiring collaboration, open-mindedness, and a willingness to take risks.

To enable innovative solutions, a culture that encourages experimentation and diverse perspectives must be cultivated. It all starts at the top: leaders should show curiosity and a willingness to explore new ideas, knowing that failure is a chance to learn and improve. They can inspire their teams to think outside the box by giving them space to try new things in a safe environment.

Leaders should also understand the needs and desires of both employees and customers by seeking feedback, engaging in conversations, and listening continuously. Taking action based on this insight is crucial. When employees see that their ideas are valued and implemented within the organization, they are more likely to be motivated and invested in the success of innovative projects.

Collaboration is like the secret sauce for coming up with cool new ideas. When you have a diverse team with different backgrounds and perspectives, you can solve problems in creative ways and come up with awesome solutions. But sometimes, leaders need to break down barriers that might be stopping their teams from working together. Everyone should have a chance to share their ideas, and those ideas should flow freely throughout the organization. This kind of teamwork not only leads to better solutions but also creates a sense of community and shared goals.

Dealing with change is another big part of making innovation happen. People are usually resistant to change because it messes with the way things are. That's why leaders need to be great communicators, be open and honest, and show empathy when guiding their teams through transitions. They need to explain why a new idea is awesome, address any concerns, and provide support to make the change happen. By giving their teams the power to figure things out and boosting their confidence, leaders can help everyone move in the right direction.

Technology is a game-changer when it comes to innovation. Leaders need to keep up with the latest tech trends and figure out how to use them to make their organization better. This might mean investing in new tools, training employees, or teaming up with experts from outside. Technology can help streamline processes, boost productivity, and open up new possibilities for growth and improvement. So, don't be afraid to embrace the tech and see where it takes you!

Innovation is an ongoing process that demands dedication, perseverance, and a forward-thinking mindset. Leaders who embrace this challenge wholeheartedly are the ones who will guide their organizations to success, creating a vibrant, dynamic, and inclusive environment for everyone to thrive.

Chapter - 13

The Future of Servant Leadership

Trends and Predictions

Leadership is evolving in a big way. It's not just about being in charge anymore - it's about showing empathy, compassion, and emotional intelligence. This shift is here to stay and will shape the future of leadership. The days of being a bossy boss are over. Now, the best leaders are the ones who lead with their hearts, understanding their team's needs and building a culture of trust and cooperation.

Remote work has only accelerated this change. With teams spread out all over the place, the old way of micromanaging just doesn't cut it anymore. Today's leaders need to be tuned in to their team's struggles and provide support that goes beyond the job. It takes a high level of emotional intelligence to pick up on your team's unspoken worries and fears and to show that you care about their well-being.

Another big trend is the focus on mental health and well-being in the workplace. Leaders are expected to create an environment where employees feel valued and supported, both professionally and personally. By fostering openness and providing support, leaders can help their teams navigate the challenges of modern life and boost engagement and productivity.

Diversity and inclusion have been a hot topic in leadership lately. Leaders are expected to be vocal about these values, making sure everyone in the workplace feels welcomed and appreciated. It's not just about having policies in place, but truly understanding and valuing the different perspectives of team members. By embracing diversity and creating an inclusive environment, leaders can unlock the full potential of their teams and boost innovation and creativity.

Technology is also changing the game for leadership. Tools like AI and data analytics give leaders new insights into team dynamics and performance. These technologies help leaders make informed decisions, address issues before they escalate, and tailor their approach to meet the needs of their team. But even with all this tech, the human touch is still crucial. Successful leaders will find a balance between using technology and connecting with their team on a personal level, using data to support an empathetic approach.

Sustainability and social responsibility are also big priorities for leaders today. It's expected that leaders will take a stand on social and environmental issues, aligning with the values of their organization and team. This means making ethical decisions, promoting sustainability, and giving back to the community. By showing a commitment to these values, leaders can inspire their teams and leave a lasting legacy of positive impact.

As leadership continues to evolve, leading with compassion will become increasingly important. Leaders who can blend empathy, emotional intelligence, and a dedication to values with utilizing technology strategically will be better equipped to navigate the complexities of the modern workplace. This is just the start of a shift towards a new style of leadership, and those who embrace it will become the benchmark for others to follow.

Adapting to a Changing World

The air was filled with the scent of opportunity as leaders, their eyes shining with curiosity and concern, entered the conference room. Outside the glass walls, the world was undergoing rapid economic, technological, and social changes. Being adaptable was not just a good quality for a leader, it was a necessity.

The room buzzed with conversations, occasionally interrupted by laughter or the clinking of coffee cups. Each leader brought with them a unique story, woven with threads of success, failure, ambition, and humility. They had gathered to discuss the future and how to navigate it from a place of authenticity.

The facilitator began by sharing a story about an organization that successfully guided its people through a period of significant change by focusing on their core values. This story set the tone for the rest of the session: connecting people during times of transformation.

The leaders were then asked to reflect on their own experiences. One executive shared how her organization transitioned to remote work. Initially, productivity plummeted and morale was low. She realized she needed to shift from micromanaging to trusting her team. By opening up dialogue and showing empathy, she was able to boost morale and productivity. Her eyes sparkled with pride as she recounted the story of the turnaround, proving that leading with heart truly makes a difference.

One leader shared his experience with a big tech upgrade. The new systems faced resistance and had a steep learning curve. He realized that success depended on the people using the technology, not just the tech itself. So, he invested in lots of training and set up a feedback forum to hear everyone's thoughts. This made the transition smoother and brought the team closer together with a shared goal.

During the discussion, the room was buzzing with ideas and strategies. Leaders talked about everything from agile methods to mindfulness. The common theme was clear: being adaptable meant balancing innovation and empathy. It wasn't enough to just react to change; you had to anticipate it and guide your team through with care.

Then, they did some exercises to boost their adaptability. They did role-play scenarios where leaders had to steer their teams through tough situations like market shifts and internal conflicts. These exercises weren't just about finding solutions; they were about understanding their team's emotions. Leaders practised active listening, emotional intelligence, and creative problem-solving - skills that would come in handy in the unpredictable world outside.

At the end of the session, the room was filled with a newfound sense of determination. Attendees not only walked away with strategies, but also a deeper understanding of their role in guiding their teams through change. They realized that adaptability isn't just about being flexible; it's about having resilience, empathy, and unwavering dedication to their people.

As the world continued to evolve outside, these leaders felt more equipped than ever to face it head-on. They had a crucial realization: leading with compassion was the key to succeeding in a constantly changing environment.

Technology and Servant Leadership

In today's fast-paced world, finding the perfect balance between technology and leadership is a top priority for many organizations. The digital age has brought us a plethora of tools designed to enhance communication, streamline processes, and aid in decision-making. However, at the heart of effective leadership lies the concept of servant leadership - the idea of truly connecting with people, showing empathy, and serving them wholeheartedly.

Integrating technology into servant leadership requires a delicate touch. While advanced tools and platforms can certainly help leaders better serve their teams, they must be used thoughtfully and purposefully. For instance, communication platforms like Slack or Microsoft Teams enable leaders to stay in touch with their teams in real-time, fostering a sense of immediacy and connection even when face-to-face interaction isn't possible. These tools can help bridge gaps and ensure that every team member feels valued and heard, regardless of their physical location.

Of course, navigating the digital landscape as a servant leader comes with its own set of challenges. The impersonal nature of digital communication can sometimes lead to misunderstandings or feelings of disconnect. To combat this, leaders can utilize videoconferencing tools to facilitate face-to-face interactions, which are crucial for building trust and rapport. Facial expressions, body language, and the nuances of tone play a vital role in effective communication, elements that can often be lost in written text.

In essence, finding the perfect balance between technology and servant leadership requires a thoughtful approach. By leveraging the benefits of technology while remaining mindful of the human element, leaders can create a more connected, engaged, and productive team.

Furthermore, technology provides new and creative ways to recognize and celebrate the accomplishments of team members. By utilizing technology, individual contributions and professional milestones are more likely to be acknowledged and promoted, fostering a culture of appreciation and motivation. Leaders can create virtual spaces where team members can share their successes and achievements, allowing others to acknowledge and validate their accomplishments, promoting a sense of community and belonging.

Data analytics is also a valuable tool that can help servant leaders better understand the needs and dynamics of their teams. By analysing patterns and trends, leaders can identify areas where their team requires additional support or resources. This proactive approach enables leaders to address issues before they escalate, demonstrating a genuine concern for the well-being of their team members.

However, leaders need to recognize the limitations of relying solely on data. While data can provide valuable insights, it cannot replace the deeper understanding that comes from personal interactions and relationships. A servant leader must ensure that decisions are informed not only by data but also by the experiences and perspectives of team members. Striking a balance between quantitative analysis and qualitative empathy is essential.

In servant leadership, technology should be seen as a tool to enhance, rather than replace, the connections between individuals. Its true power is realized when technology amplifies the core principles of servant leadership: empathy, support, and empowerment. Leaders can leverage technological tools to foster a heart-centred approach, creating an environment where team members feel valued, understood, and motivated to achieve their full potential.

Servant leadership paired with technology can be tricky, but with some strategic applications, it can enhance a leader's ability to serve effectively. In a world that is becoming more digitally focused, it's important to prioritize human connections and empathy to embody the essence of servant leadership and guide teams to success and fulfilment.

Global Perspectives

In today's interconnected world, leading with heart has a whole new meaning. Leaders need to look beyond their local and national boundaries to understand the complexities of global dynamics. Leading with heart means respecting and understanding different perspectives from around the world, regardless of cultural or geographical differences.

It's not just about acknowledging diversity, but embracing it and incorporating it into leadership practices. Successful global leaders have cultural intelligence, allowing them to connect with others from different backgrounds with empathy and understanding. This requires a commitment to continuously learning about various cultures, traditions, and worldviews.

Global leadership also requires an understanding of the social, economic, and political landscapes in which businesses operate. Leaders need to stay informed about global trends, such as economic changes, technological advancements, social movements, and environmental issues. By being aware of these trends, leaders can prepare for potential threats and take advantage of opportunities to keep their organizations strong and adaptable in a rapidly changing world.

Overall, leading with heart in a global context is a crucial area of study for leaders looking to navigate the complexities of our interconnected world.

To be a successful global leader, it's crucial to prioritize inclusivity and equality. This means making sure that everyone's voice is heard and valued, no matter where they come from. Embracing diversity not only boosts creativity and innovation but also strengthens teams, making them better equipped to navigate the complexities of the global market.

Another key aspect of global leadership is effective communication. Leaders need to be able to convey their vision and values across different cultures and languages. This goes beyond just speaking the language - it's about being sensitive to different communication styles and showing respect for diversity. Good global leaders listen actively and empathetically, fostering open communication and mutual respect.

Ethical considerations are also a big part of global leadership. Leaders operating in diverse cultural and regulatory environments must act with integrity and show respect for human dignity. By doing so, they can build trust and credibility within their organizations and the global community as a whole.

Furthermore, today's leaders need to be able to foster and maintain international relationships. This is crucial for driving innovation, expanding market opportunities, and addressing pressing global issues such as climate change and social inequality. In today's interconnected world, leaders must adopt a collective mindset as many challenges can no longer be solved within the confines of one country's borders. Collaboration among nations is key.

In the realm of global leadership, adaptability and resilience are also vital. Leaders must be able to navigate uncertainties and complexities on a global scale, adjust strategies as needed, and bounce back from setbacks with determination. Cultivating a culture of adaptability within organizations is essential for success in a rapidly changing global landscape.

Leading with compassion and empathy is another important aspect of global leadership. This involves having a strong understanding of different cultures, maintaining ethical standards, communicating effectively, and promoting inclusivity and collaboration. Leaders who embody these qualities can inspire and guide their teams towards success while also contributing to the betterment of the global community.

Sustaining Servant Leadership Practices

Servant leadership isn't just about being super enthusiastic - it's about sticking to the principles of empathy and humility. You are going to listen to people if you want to keep up with this kind of leadership. Leaders need to make sure these values are at the heart of everything they do.

The key to keeping up with servant leadership is self-awareness. Leaders need to think about their actions, intentions, and how they affect others. This helps them spot when they start slipping into more traditional, bossy styles of leadership. Getting feedback from colleagues and team members can also give some good insights into how to improve.

Building a community of like-minded leaders is also important. It's great to have people to share challenges and successes with. This can be anything from formal workshops to just chatting with peers.

And don't forget to keep learning and growing. Leadership is always changing, so it's good to stay up to date with new ideas and techniques. Going to seminars, reading up on leadership, and training sessions can all help. Putting new ideas into practice can help keep that servant leadership spirit alive.

Encouraging a culture of servant leadership within an organization can help promote sustainability. This means instilling values from the top down and making them a part of the organization's ethos. When leaders take responsibility for their team members' growth and development, it fosters empathy, humility, and selflessness among the team. Recognizing and rewarding these behaviours can further reinforce the practice of servant leadership.

It's important to find a balance between personal and professional life. Servant leaders often invest a lot emotionally and mentally in their roles, which can lead to burnout if not managed properly. Practising self-care by setting boundaries and taking time to rest and rejuvenate is crucial for sustaining effective leadership.

Technology can also support servant leadership practices. Communication, project management, and feedback tools can enhance empathetic and responsive interactions. For example, video conferencing check-ins can maintain a personal touch in remote teams, while feedback tools provide real-time insights into morale and engagement.

Celebrating small wins and milestones is equally important. This helps boost morale and reinforces the value of servant leadership. Celebrations can be as simple as acknowledgments at meetings, personal notes of appreciation, or more formal recognitions during organizational events.

In the end, it's all about maintaining servant leadership by constantly reflecting, learning, and adapting to foster an environment where these principles can flourish. By implementing these practices, leaders can seamlessly integrate them into their daily routines and cultivate a culture that provides the necessary support to remain dedicated to serving with resilience.

Chapter - 14

Measuring the Impact of Servant Leadership

Key Performance Indicators

When it comes to leadership, it's important to be able to measure progress and success. One key element in efficient leadership is using Key Performance Indicators (KPIs). These are like navigation tools that help leaders manage their organizations and stay on track with their goals.

KPIs are measurable values that show how well an organization is performing. They are carefully chosen to represent the most important factors for success in a business. By using KPIs, leaders can track progress, achieve objectives, and move closer to long-term goals. KPIs help turn big ideas into concrete results.

Choosing the right KPIs is crucial. Leaders need to understand what matters most to their organization's mission, vision, and goals. Effective KPIs are specific, measurable, achievable, relevant, and time-bound (SMART). This ensures that each KPI aligns with the organization's objectives and can be realistically achieved within a set timeframe. Leaders also need to balance financial and non-financial indicators to get a complete picture of performance.

Overall, using KPIs is a smart way for leaders to stay focused, track progress, and make informed decisions to drive their organizations forward.

Financial KPIs are like the health check-up for a company. They show how much money is coming in, how much profit is being made, and how well investments are paying off. However, relying only on these numbers can hold a business back. Non-financial KPIs, like how happy customers are, how engaged employees are, and how innovative a company is, are just as important for success. These indicators can reveal issues that financial metrics might miss.

One challenge for leaders is keeping up with changing conditions. What works as a key performance indicator today might not matter tomorrow. Leaders need to constantly review and update their KPIs to stay on track with their goals and adapt to new challenges.

Implementing KPIs also means creating a culture of accountability and transparency. Leaders need to make sure their teams understand the importance of these indicators and how their work contributes to the overall goals of the organization. Regular reporting and analysis of KPIs can help teams improve and grow stronger over time.

Secondly, KPIs are super important because they help leaders make decisions based on facts. This means they can be more objective and not just go with their gut feelings. Having solid data to back up decisions helps get rid of any bias and gives more weight to the choices leaders make. When leaders have concrete data to support their decisions, it builds trust and confidence with everyone involved, showing that they're committed to being open and accountable.

In the book Leading with Heart, they stress the importance of KPIs in showing how successful an organization is. KPIs aren't just random numbers on a screen; they're a key part of the bigger picture of where the organization is headed. By picking the right KPIs, putting them into action effectively, and constantly improving them, leaders can set their organization up for long-term success by making their goals both inspiring and achievable.

Qualitative Assessments

When it comes to leadership, the heartbeat of an organization is all about the experiences, emotions, and values of the people involved. It's not just about the numbers and stats - leaders need to dig deeper into the qualitative aspects that make up the teams and culture. This means listening to stories, watching interactions, and picking up on those subtle signals that you might miss if you're just looking at data.

Qualitative assessment is the art of really listening. It's about tuning into the emotions and motivations behind people's actions, not just the words they're saying. Leaders who can master this skill will gain insights that go beyond the surface. For example, in a one-on-one chat where someone expresses concerns about a project, a perceptive leader can pick up on cues like tone of voice, body language, and choice of words to uncover deeper issues like lack of confidence or tension among team members.

Another important aspect is observing how team members interact with each other. This can reveal communication patterns, collaboration styles, and potential conflicts. A leader might notice that some people dominate conversations while others stay quiet, indicating an imbalance that needs to be addressed. By creating an inclusive environment where everyone feels valued and heard, leaders can foster a more productive team dynamic.

Understanding qualitative signals requires a mix of empathy and analytical thinking. Empathy helps leaders connect with their team on a personal level, while analytical thinking helps them make sense of what they observe. For example, if a leader notices that team morale is low due to tight deadlines, they can use empathy to understand the stress and analytical thinking to figure out how to improve productivity and boost morale.

Storytelling is a powerful tool in qualitative assessments. Stories can make complex ideas more relatable and memorable. By encouraging team members to share their experiences, leaders can gain valuable insights into the organization's challenges and successes. These stories can also inspire and motivate the team to work towards common goals.

Creating a culture of openness and honesty is essential for effective qualitative assessments. Leaders need to make sure team members feel comfortable sharing their thoughts and feelings without fear of judgment. Regular check-ins, opportunities for anonymous feedback, and addressing concerns are all ways to foster this culture. When team members feel heard and respected, they are more likely to provide valuable insights that can lead to positive changes.

Qualitative assessment isn't just a one-time thing; it's an ongoing process. Teams and organizations are always changing, so new challenges and opportunities are always popping up. By staying aware of the qualitative aspects of their leadership, leaders can adapt and respond to these changes with agility and compassion. Keeping in touch with the human side of leadership keeps the organization lively and strong.

On the other hand, qualitative assessments help support the overall health and vitality of an organization. They can dive deep into the relationships, emotions, and values that make successful teams tick. Leaders who lead with heart and embrace these assessments can create a culture of empathy, trust, and collaboration that leads to long-term success.

Feedback from Team Members
When it comes to managing teams, leaders often rely on feedback from team members to navigate the complexities. This feedback is crucial because it provides insight into the group's collective mindset, highlighting both strengths and areas for improvement. It serves as a reflection of the leader's effectiveness and the team's dynamics, giving a true picture of the workplace environment.

In the hustle to meet targets and deadlines, leaders can lose touch with their team's experiences. Feedback acts as a bridge, reconnecting them to the realities on the frontline. When team members feel heard, it fosters a sense of belonging and loyalty. They become more engaged, knowing their voices shape the team's direction. This creates a culture of trust, where open communication thrives, and innovation flourishes.

Effective feedback is a two-way street. It's not just about receiving input but also taking action on it. When team members see their ideas implemented or concerns addressed, it reinforces their belief that the leader values them. This action-oriented approach turns feedback into tangible improvements, fostering proactive and responsive leadership.

Collecting feedback is an art that requires sensitivity and skill. Leaders must create an environment where people feel safe to speak up without fear of reprisal. Building a culture of psychological safety encourages growth through vulnerability. Regular check-ins, anonymous surveys, and an open-door policy are tools that can elicit honest and constructive feedback.

Feedback can cover a wide range of topics, from interpersonal relationships to operational efficiencies. Some people might mention issues with workload distribution, while others could point out communication gaps or the need for more resources. Leaders must be able to identify common themes and address them as a whole. This requires empathy and the ability to prioritize what will have the greatest impact.

Feedback isn't just about pointing out mistakes. Positive feedback is just as important, if not more so. Recognizing and celebrating achievements, big or small, boosts morale and reinforces positive behaviors. It shows team members that their efforts are valued and appreciated, motivating others to strive for excellence as well.

Leaders also benefit from receiving feedback on their own performance. It can be humbling but also enlightening to hear how your actions are perceived by your team. This feedback is crucial for personal growth and effective leadership, setting an example for continuous improvement.

Leading with heart means being open to feedback from your team. The process of giving and receiving feedback involves active listening, empathy, and a willingness to make changes. By valuing and acting on feedback, leaders can build stronger, more cohesive teams that can tackle challenges and seize opportunities.

Long-term Success Stories

Success stories in the corporate world serve as beacons of hope and inspiration. These stories go beyond just achieving financial milestones; they are about creating a space where values, vision, and humanity come together in a supportive environment. One such inspiring success story is that of Patagonia, an organization that prioritizes environmental responsibility and ethical business practices. Their commitment has not only led to financial success but also to a loyal and passionate customer base. Patagonia's focus on putting the planet and people first shows that true success is about more than just making a profit.

Another standout example is Southwest Airlines, known for its exceptional customer service and high employee satisfaction. The leadership at Southwest believes in taking care of their people, treating them well, and valuing them as important stakeholders. This focus on creating a culture of respect and inclusion has empowered employees to provide outstanding experiences for customers. Maintaining this culture for decades highlights the lasting impact of leading with empathy and integrity.

Unilever's long-term success is another testament to purposeful leadership. Under the guidance of leaders like Paul Polman, Unilever has embraced a sustainable business model that balances profit with social and environmental responsibility. By integrating sustainability into its core strategy, Unilever has not only reduced its ecological footprint but also earned consumer trust and loyalty through ethical business practices. Aligning corporate objectives with societal values has positioned Unilever as a leader in both enterprise performance and corporate social responsibility.

Starbucks is not just a coffee shop - it's a place where heart-centered leadership principles are at the core. Howard Schultz had a vision to create a space between work and home where people could come together and relax. Today, Starbucks is a global sensation, known for its commitment to fair trade, community involvement, and employee benefits. This dedication has made customers and employees feel like they belong, helping

Starbucks weather economic ups and downs and remain one of the most beloved brands worldwide.

When it comes to technology, Salesforce stands out for its philanthropic efforts. Since its inception, Salesforce has integrated giving into its business model through Marc Benioff's 1-1-1 model. This approach involves dedicating 1% of the organization's equity, product, and employee time to charitable initiatives. By prioritizing making a difference, Salesforce has not only engaged employees but also attracted clients and partners who share similar values, creating a ripple effect that drives growth and innovation.

These stories show how leading with heart can have a significant impact. They highlight that long-term success isn't just about strategy or market position, but about creating a culture centred on values, purpose, and human connections. Leaders who prioritize their employees, communities, and the environment create organizations that are resilient, adaptable, and sustainable in the long run. Their examples remind us that true leadership goes beyond traditional metrics, focusing on the essence of human progress and aspiration.

Continuous Improvement

Being an excellent leader requires absolute dedication and a strong desire for growth. Leaders who are committed to constantly improving understand that progress is a journey, not a destination. They create an environment where feedback is not only accepted but actively sought out and embraced. By fostering a culture of learning and adaptation, these leaders motivate their teams to strive for excellence in all aspects of their work.

At the heart of continuous improvement is the belief that there is always room for improvement, innovation, and growth. Leaders with this mindset are constantly questioning and challenging existing processes, encouraging their teams to do the same. They create a culture where trying new approaches and taking calculated risks is the norm, driving innovation and empowering their team members to take ownership of their development.

Feedback plays a crucial role in continuous improvement. Great leaders see feedback as a valuable gift that provides insight into their strengths and areas for growth. They actively seek feedback from colleagues, subordinates, and mentors, recognizing that diverse perspectives can uncover blind spots and spark new ideas. By demonstrating a positive attitude towards feedback, leaders set the tone for their teams, showing that constructive criticism is a learning opportunity, not a personal attack.

For feedback to be truly effective, it needs to be actionable. Leaders must be able to take that feedback and turn it into real actions for improvement. This involves setting SMART goals, creating a plan to achieve those goals, having regular check-ins, and monitoring progress to ensure we stay on track. Celebrating small wins along the way helps to keep us motivated and moving forward.

Continuous improvement also requires a thirst for knowledge and growth. Leaders should seek out learning opportunities, whether through formal education, training, mentorship, or self-teaching. The more we know about our industry and best practices, the better equipped we are to bring new ideas and innovative thinking to our teams. By continuing to learn, we set an example of lifelong learning for those around us.

Adaptability is another key ingredient for continuous improvement. The world is always changing, so being able to adjust our strategies in response to new information and circumstances is crucial. Leaders in continuous improvement are flexible, resilient, and able to navigate uncertainty to turn challenges into opportunities. By fostering a culture of embracing change, we can help our teams grow and evolve.

Continuous improvement is all about striving for excellence in leadership. It's about always looking for ways to lead better, inspire others, and reach our goals. Leaders who are dedicated to continuous improvement create a lively and successful atmosphere where everyone can reach their full potential. They do this by fostering a culture of feedback, learning, and adaptation that not only improves their own effectiveness but also boosts their team's performance and satisfaction. By leading with passion, they ensure that the journey to excellence is rewarding and long-lasting.

Chapter - 15

Conclusion and Next Steps

Recap of Key Concepts

Leading with Heart takes a deep dive into the significant impact that emotional intelligence, empathy, and authenticity have on our leadership abilities. It offers a fresh perspective on how leaders can create a strong connection with their team, fostering an environment where trust and collaboration can flourish. This book encourages us to lead not just with our minds, but with our hearts, urging us to be compassionate, inclusive, and authentically human in our approach.

Reflecting on the foundational principles discussed, we come back to the essence of leading - emotional intelligence. This term refers to our ability to understand and manage our own emotions, as well as those of others. According to Daniel Goleman, emotional intelligence can be broken down into four parts: self-awareness, self-management, social awareness, and relationship management. Each of these components plays a crucial role in a leader's ability to connect with their team on a deeper level.

Self-awareness is the cornerstone of emotional intelligence. It involves having a clear understanding of our own emotions, strengths, weaknesses, values, and motivations. Leaders with high self-awareness not only recognize their emotions but also understand how those emotions influence their thoughts and actions. This self-awareness allows them to make sound decisions, stay grounded, and maintain perspective, even in challenging situations."

Self-management is all about being aware of yourself and knowing how to handle your emotions and behaviour in different situations. It's about being resilient and adaptable when faced with challenges. Leaders who are good at self-management can handle stress, stay positive, and inspire confidence in their team. They show self-control and honesty, creating an environment where everyone feels safe to be themselves.

Social awareness is about looking beyond yourself and focusing on understanding and empathizing with others. It's about being able to pick up on other people's emotions, needs, and concerns. People with social awareness can read social cues and navigate relationships with ease. They genuinely care about their team members and foster a culture of acceptance and respect.

Relationship management is all about building and maintaining strong relationships. This is a crucial aspect of being a successful leader, as it involves clear communication, conflict resolution, and the ability to motivate and influence others. Leaders with strong relationship management skills connect deeply with their team, build trust, promote teamwork, and inspire everyone to work together towards common goals. They positively handle conflicts, ensuring that differences strengthen relationships rather than divide them.

The book hammers home the importance of authentic leadership. An Authentic leader stays true to themselves and their values, always leading with integrity and consistency. They're open, honest, and transparent, which helps build trust and credibility. When leaders are authentic, they create a safe space for their teams to be themselves and take risks without fear of judgment.

Another big theme in the book is empathy. It means being able to put yourself in someone else's shoes and understand what they're feeling. An empathetic leader can sense the emotions of those around them and know when a team member needs some encouragement or reassurance. This kind of connection helps teams feel like they belong and stay motivated.

Leading with your heart isn't about tasks and deadlines; it's about nurturing the human spirit at work. Emotional intelligence, empathy, and authenticity are key ways for leaders to create a positive environment where people feel valued, heard, and able to bring their best selves to the table.

Personal Action Plan

As a heart-centred leader, it's important to create a personal action plan that looks back and forward at the same time. This plan should be rooted in authenticity and guided by values that feel truly compelling. It's not just a simple to-do list, but a thoughtful roadmap that aligns personal growth with professional goals.

Start by taking a good look at yourself. Reflect on your strengths, weaknesses, and what makes you a leader. What matters to you? How can these aspects align with your leadership aspirations? This self-awareness will form the foundation of your action plan and help you see things more clearly.

Next, set clear goals that reflect your values and can be measured and achieved within a specific timeframe. For example, if creating a collaborative team environment is a priority, outline the steps needed to improve communication and trust within your team. Break these tasks down into smaller, meaningful steps that lead to your larger goal.

Regular self-reflection is key to staying on track. Take time to review your progress, celebrate your achievements, and identify areas for improvement. This will help you maintain a growth mindset, allowing you to adapt and refine your leadership approach as needed in response to changing circumstances.

Get feedback from people you trust, like your colleagues and mentors. Their input can give you a fresh perspective and point out any blind spots you might have missed. Constructive feedback is key to personal growth; it's a chance to learn and improve yourself. Be open to feedback, use it to guide your actions, and make any necessary changes.

Make learning a continuous habit in your leadership journey. Stay up-to-date on new theories, trends, and best practices in your field. Attend workshops, read the latest research, and explore relevant literature to further your professional development. A commitment to learning will enhance your skills and demonstrate your dedication to excellence.

Balance is crucial in your action plan. Set realistic goals and tasks that are manageable. Avoid overloading yourself with tasks to prevent burnout. Find a balance that allows you to prioritize your well-being while still achieving your leadership goals. This balance will lead to long-term success and fulfilment.

Build a supportive network with individuals who share your vision and values. Collaborate with peers who can provide inspiration, advice, and accountability. These connections will keep you motivated, focused, and resilient when faced with challenges.

Celebrate all your wins, big or small! Take a moment to pat yourself on the back and appreciate the progress you're making. These celebrations are a great reminder of how you can inspire others through your leadership and keep that fire burning inside you.

Stay open to change and be ready to adapt. The leadership game is always changing, so make sure your plan can roll with the punches. Stay curious, keep innovating, and always be on the lookout for ways to grow and get better.

Create a personal action plan that speaks to your heart and work towards those goals with passion. Leading with authenticity and purpose will not only help you grow as a leader but also create a positive and inspiring environment for your team. Keep pushing forward and watch your leadership skills soar!

Resources for Further Learning

If you're all about leading with heart, there are plenty of resources out there to help you on your journey. From books and articles to podcasts and courses, there's a wide range of insights and perspectives to inspire and guide you towards a more empathetic and effective style of leadership.

Books are a great way to deepen your knowledge in this area. Classics like The Servant as Leader by Kumar K. Greenleaf explore the philosophy of servant leadership, emphasizing the importance of serving others as a key aspect of leadership. Dare to Lead by Brené Brown is another must-read, offering advice on how to lead with courage and vulnerability authentically. Brown's research-backed insights can help you build trust and foster a culture of openness and empathy within your team.

If you prefer a more narrative approach, check out Leaders Eat Last by Simon Sinek. This book is full of stories and case studies that show how leaders can create an environment where people feel valued and motivated. Sinek digs into the biological and anthropological roots of leadership, making a compelling case for why leading with heart is not just beneficial, but essential for long-term success.

Have you ever thought about how emotional intelligence and empathy can impact organizational performance? Well, articles and academic papers are a great way to dive into this topic. Journals like the Harvard Business Review regularly publish articles on emotional intelligence, empathy in leadership, and how they affect how well a company does. For example, Daniel Goleman's article "What Makes a Leader?" breaks down emotional intelligence and how it plays a role in successful leadership.

If reading isn't your thing, podcasts are a fun and easy way to learn about leadership. Shows like The Dare to Lead Podcast with Brené Brown feature interviews with experts who share their experiences and insights on leading with heart. The Tony Robbins Podcast is another great option for diving into the emotional and mental side of leadership, offering practical tips and tools for listeners to use on their leadership journey.

For those who prefer a more structured approach to learning, online classes and workshops are a fantastic option. Websites like Coursera and LinkedIn Learning offer courses on emotional intelligence, leadership development, and mindfulness in leadership. For example, the course "Leading with Emotional Intelligence" by Case Western Reserve University on Coursera combines theory with hands-on exercises to help leaders enhance their empathetic leadership skills.

In addition to those sources, reaching out to professional networks and communities can provide even more support and encouragement. Events hosted by organizations like the Center for Creative Leadership and the International Leadership Association offer webinars and forums where leaders can come together to share stories and learn from one another. Getting involved in these communities not only expands your knowledge but also allows you to connect with like-minded individuals who are passionate about leading with compassion.

Incorporating these resources into your leadership development plan can have profound benefits. By continuously learning and being open to new ideas, you can adopt a more empathetic and authentic approach to leadership. Exploring heart-centred leadership through various mediums such as reading, listening, studying, and discussing different perspectives is a fulfilling and transformative journey.

Encouragement and Motivation

In the somewhat boring office, the smell of freshly brewed coffee mixed with the faint scent of wood polish to create a vibe of leadership. Being a leader goes beyond just telling people what to do; it's about inspiring, creating a sense of belonging, and keeping everyone motivated and valued. The key to good leadership is to encourage and motivate your team. Encouragement comes from recognizing and appreciating each team member's strengths. It's like a delicate dance of words and actions that need to be genuine. Imagine a leader watching a hardworking employee putting in extra effort on a tough project. Instead of just saying "good job," the leader takes the time to point out specific things like late nights and creative solutions. This kind of recognition not only shows that the employee's efforts are appreciated, but also boosts their confidence in their role within the team.

Motivation is what pushes people to reach their goals; it's that fire that keeps them going. A good leader knows that different team members are motivated by different things.

Some thrive on challenges, others on growth opportunities, and some on feeling like they're part of something bigger. By understanding what motivates each team member, a leader can create a path for the team to follow.

Imagine this as the tale of a young professional facing challenges in a new role. The boss, sensing the struggle, takes the time to sit down and listen. He opens up about his doubts and growth, painting a picture of progress. By showing vulnerability, the boss not only builds trust but also inspires hope and resilience in the young professional. The message is clear: obstacles are just stepping stones, not roadblocks.

When it comes to encouragement and motivation, actions speak louder than words. A leader who jumps in to work alongside the team sends a powerful message of solidarity and dedication. Whether it's staying late to meet a deadline or offering support during a crisis, these actions create a culture of respect and shared responsibility.

The physical workspace also plays a crucial role in motivation. A vibrant, inclusive environment that reflects the team's values can boost morale. Picture a common area filled with motivational quotes, success stories, and reminders of past achievements and future goals. These surroundings serve as constant reminders of the team's potential and what they can achieve together.

Encouragement and motivation are not just tools for a leader, but the lifeblood that keeps the team's spirit alive. They transform a group of individuals into a united team with a shared vision and purpose. A leader can create an environment where each team member feels seen, heard, and inspired to give their best through genuine recognition, personalized motivation, and leading by example. It's in this nurturing setting that potential blossoms and true leadership thrives.

Final Thoughts

Leading with heart isn't just a strategy - it's a way of life. The lessons and experiences gathered along the way shine brightly on the horizon as the sun sets on the vast landscape of leadership. It's about finding strength in vulnerability, staying true to yourself, and making a real impact through empathy.

When you take a moment to reflect, you can see the intricate tapestry woven from moments of courage and compassion. Each thread tells a story of resilience, with the leader's heart acting as both a compass and an anchor. Challenges aren't roadblocks, but opportunities to dig deeper into empathy and understanding. Every decision and interaction becomes a testament to the power of leading with heart.

It's all about forming connections that go beyond the surface. It's about seeing others as individuals with dreams, fears, and aspirations, rather than just pieces in a puzzle. This new way of leading changes the game, fostering trust, respect, and innovation, and celebrating achievements together with pure joy.

A leader who leads from the heart understands the power of simply being present. It's in those moments of connection that true bonds are formed. Whether you're actively listening, offering words of comfort, or recognizing someone's hard work, those small gestures can inspire others to lead with compassion and integrity.

Leading with a heart also means being committed to self-improvement. It's about facing your biases and limitations head-on, seeking out different perspectives, and embracing the discomfort of growth. The path isn't straight and narrow, but full of twists and turns that shape you into a more authentic leader.

The concept of leading with heart is a timeless principle that remains relevant even as the landscape of leadership evolves. It serves as a reminder that effective leadership is rooted in a profound understanding of humanity. This understanding gives us the desire to make a positive impact, uplift others, and leave a lasting mark on the world. A heart-led leader's legacy is not defined by awards or job titles but by the lives they have touched and the communities they have strengthened.

In today's rapidly changing world, the call to lead from the heart grows louder. It urges individuals to rise above the noise, embrace empathy and compassion, and prioritize the well-being of all. As leaders navigate the complexities of their roles, they should always remember the guiding principle that the heart is not just a physical organ, but a source of boundless strength and wisdom.

Leading with the heart is a journey of continuous growth and discovery. It promises deeper connections, greater fulfilment, and a more meaningful impact. As leaders embark on this path, they should keep in mind that true leadership is not about intellect alone, but about the compassion and empathy that reside in the heart.

References

1. The Servant as Leader by Kumar K. Greenleaf
2. The Monday Memo from John Stanko
3. King Asoka as a Role Model of Buddhist Leadership by Thomas Voss.
4. Evaluating Historical Views of Leadership by James Martin
5. Leadership Lessons from the Mahabharata by Rajdeep D
6. Romans 1:1–16. Introduction. Paul As Servant-leader
7. My Life in Full by Indra Nooyi
8. Servant leadership – Everything you need to know by Jason Evanish, CEO
9. Salesforce equality article – Salesforce website
10. The 4 CEOs created a new standard of leadership by Bull George
11. Servant leadership in education -Keiser University
12. Montessori Literature Through the Lens of Leadership by Jane Bone
13. The Man and Era -Soviet psychologist Lev Vygotsky
14. Servant-Leadership in a Changing Culture by R Marinho, J Arrais

www.ingramcontent.com/pod-product-compliance
Lightning Source LLC
LaVergne TN
LVHW061343080526
838199LV00093B/6925